*Abraham Lincoln
and the Second American Revolution*

ABRAHAM

LINCOLN

and the Second American Revolution

JAMES M. McPHERSON

New York   Oxford   OXFORD UNIVERSITY PRESS

Oxford University Press

Oxford   New York   Toronto
Delhi   Bombay   Calcutta   Madras   Karachi
Kuala Lumpur   Singapore   Hong Kong   Tokyo
Nairobi   Dar es Salaam   Cape Town
Melbourne   Auckland

and associated companies in
Berlin   Ibadan

Copyright © 1991 by James M. McPherson

First published in 1991 by Oxford University Press, Inc.,
198 Madison Avenue, New York, New York 10016-4314

First issued as an Oxford University Press paperback, 1992

Oxford is a registered trademark of Oxford University Press

All rights reserved. No part of this publication may be reproduced,
stored in a retrieval system, or transmitted, in any form or by any means,
electronic, mechanical, photocopying, recording, or otherwise,
without the prior permission of Oxford University Press, Inc.

Library of Congress Cataloging-in-Publication Data
McPherson, James M.
Abraham Lincoln and the Second American Revolution
James M. McPherson.
p.   cm.   Includes bibliographical references.
1. Lincoln, Abraham, 1809–1865—Military leadership.
2. United States–History–Civil War, 1861–1865–Influence.
I. Title.   E457.2.M4758   1991
973.7'092–dc20   90–6885

ISBN 0–19–505542–X
ISBN 0–19–507606–0 (pbk.)

20 19 18 17 16

Printed in the United States of America

To Pat and Jenny
with love and appreciation

Preface

Four years after the guns fell silent at Appomattox, Harvard historian George Ticknor reflected on the meaning of the Civil War. That national trauma had riven "a great gulf between what happened before in our century and what has happened since, or what is likely to happen hereafter. It does not seem to me as if I were living in the country in which I was born."[1]

Ticknor had been born in 1791, during the third year of George Washington's presidency, in a country still basking in the glow of the Revolution that had given it birth. He had lived through eighteen presidential administrations and a Second American Revolution that gave the United States "a new birth of freedom" during the administration of its sixteenth president. This is a book about that president and the revolution he led, which so utterly transformed the nation that George Ticknor could scarcely recognize it. Nor could a Louisiana planter who returned home after four years as an officer in the Confederate army to discover that "society has been completely changed by the war. The [French] revolution of '89 did not produce a greater change in the 'Ancien Regime' than has this in our social life."[2]

Abraham Lincoln was not Maximilien de Robespierre. No Confederate leaders went to the guillotine. Yet the Civil War changed the United States as thoroughly as the French Revolution changed that country. The liberation of four million slaves, along with destruction of the South's political domination of national affairs and of the social order on which that domination was founded, metamorphosed a region (the former slave states) more than three times as large as France. The future of America after 1865 belonged to a system of democratic free-labor capitalism, not one of slave-labor plantation agriculture. The House Divided of 1858 was no longer divided. Liberty took on new meanings for Americans. The old decentralized federal republic became a new national polity that taxed the people directly, created an internal revenue bureau to collect these taxes, expanded the jurisdiction of federal courts, established a national currency and a national banking structure.

The United States went to war in 1861 to preserve the *Union;* it emerged from war in 1865 having created a *nation*. Before 1861 the two words "United States" were generally used as a plural noun: "the United States *are* a republic." After 1865 the United States became a singular noun. The loose union of states became a nation. Lincoln's wartime speeches marked this transition. In his first inaugural address he mentioned the "Union" twenty times but the nation not once. In his first message to Congress, on July 4, 1861, Lincoln used the word "Union" thirty-two times and "nation" only three times. But in his Gettysburg Address two and one-half years later, the president did not mention the Union at all but spoke of the "nation" five times to invoke a new birth of freedom and nationhood. And in his second inaugural address on March 4, 1865, Lincoln spoke of the South seeking to dissolve the Union in 1861 and the North accepting the challenge to preserve the nation.

The seven essays that follow examine these events from several perspectives. The first and last analyze the scope and meaning of revolutionary transformations in both substance and process wrought by the Civil War. The other five treat various aspects of Lincoln's leadership in accomplishing these changes. The essays originated as lectures or papers to audiences ranging from fellow historians to that indistinct but real entity, the "general public." Each essay can stand alone and be read separately. They also cohere in a pattern that develops variations on the two themes expressed in the title. Because they examine different facets of these themes, looking at them from one angle and then another to catch different qualities of light, the careful reader of all seven essays may discern slight overlaps in evidence and interpretation. In revising the essays for this volume, I have tried to eliminate unnecessary duplication among them while retaining enough substance in each that it can stand on its own. I hope that readers will find new insights in each essay and will also conclude that the whole equals the sum of its parts.

More than thirty years ago, historian David Herbert Donald noted the compulsion that American public figures feel to "get right with Lincoln"—to square their own position with what they suppose Lincoln would have done in similar circumstances, or to find a Lincoln quotation that allegedly supports their present attitude on almost any issue under the sun.[3] I have had personal experience with this remarkable hold that Lincoln has on the American imagination. On the 175th anniversary of Lincoln's birth in 1984, I delivered a version of the title essay of this volume to the Lincoln Club of Delaware, whose members included the governor, the chief justice of the state supreme court, and other political leaders. After my talk, a reporter for a Wilmington radio station taped an interview with me. His first question was: "If Lincoln were alive today, what position would be take on abortion and the budget deficit?"

I do not pretend to know where Lincoln's philosophy of liberty—the subject of one of the essays in this book—would have led him on the abortion issue. But his ideas and actions on the subjects of slavery, freedom, civil liberties, power, nationalism, and presidential leadership are as interesting and perhaps as relevant today as they were a century and a quarter ago. The enthusiastic sponsorship by the Solidarity party in Poland of a translation of Lincoln's writings on democracy into the Polish language, and plans for similar translations into other eastern European languages, testifies to the enduring significance of Lincoln's words and ideas.[4] The issues that Lincoln grappled with will never become obsolete: the meaning of freedom; the limits of government power and individual liberty in time of crisis; the dimensions of democracy; the nature of nationalism; the problems of leadership in war and peace; the tragedies and triumphs of a revolutionary civil war. I hope the essays that follow will focus fresh light on these matters.

Princeton
March 1990

James M. McPherson

Acknowledgments

It is a pleasure to acknowledge the encouragement, assistance, and constructive criticism of the following individuals who invited me to deliver lectures or papers that constituted the initial versions of these essays, or offered suggestions for their improvement: Michael Les Benedict of the Ohio State University; Gabor Boritt of Gettysburg College; LaWanda Cox of Hunter College; Richard N. Current of the University of North Carolina at Greensboro; Don E. Fehrenbacher of Stanford University; Leslie H. Fishel of the Rutherford B. Hayes Presidential Center; Maldwyn Jones of University College, London; Robert Kaczorowski of Fordham University Law School; Mark E. Neely, Jr., of the Louis A. Warren Lincoln Library and Museum; Peter Parish of the Institute of American History in London; John Phillip Reid of the New York University Law School and the Huntington Library; Martin Ridge of the Huntington Library; Thomas F. Schwarz of the Abraham Lincoln Association; Lawrence Stone of the Shelby Cullom Davis Center at Princeton University; John L. Thomas of Brown University; and Frank J. Williams of the Abraham Lincoln Association. I am especially grateful to the Center for Advanced Study in the Behavioral Sciences at Stanford and the National Endowment for the Humanities, and the Henry E. Huntington Library in San Marino and the Seaver Institute, which provided wonderful facilities and financial support for two sabbatical years in California during which part of the research and writing of these essays went forward. A week's sojourn in London as the Commonwealth Fund Lecturer in American History also offered stimulating feedback on some of the ideas that appear in this book. Members of the Shelby Cullom Davis Center at Princeton University and of the Symposium on Emancipation and Its Aftermath sponsored by the Graduate Center of the City University of New York make useful criticisms and suggestions. Sheldon Meyer and Leona Capeless of Oxford University Press have expertly guided the book through the publication process. My wife Patricia McPherson has, as always, given of her love and endured in patience while sitting through the lectures—sometimes more than once—that with her help and advice eventually matured into the essays that follow.

I am grateful to the following for permission to reprint earlier versions of these essays:

Rutherford B. Hayes Presidential Center
"The Second American Revolution," in *Hayes Historical Journal* 3 (Spring 1982).

University of Massachusetts Press
"Abraham Lincoln and the Second American Revolution," in *Abraham Lincoln and the American Political Tradition,* ed. John L. Thomas (1986).

The Henry E. Huntington Library
"Lincoln and Liberty," in *Essays in the History of Liberty: Seaver Institute Lectures at the Huntington Library* (1988).

Gettysburg College
Lincoln and the Strategy of Unconditional Surrender, 23rd Annual Robert Fortenbaugh Memorial Lecture, 1984.

The Louis A. Warren Lincoln Library and Museum
"How Lincoln Won the War with Metaphors,"
Eighth Annual R. Gerald McMurtry Lecture, 1985.

The Abraham Lincoln Association
"The Hedgehog and the Foxes: Lincoln and Some
Contemporaries," in *Journal of the Abraham Lincoln
Association* 12 (1991).

Contents

*Abraham Lincoln
and the Second American Revolution*

I   *The Second American Revolution*

During the fateful years of 1860 and 1861, James A. Garfield, a representative in the Ohio legislature, corresponded with his former student at Hiram College, Burke Hinsdale, about the alarming developments in national affairs. They agreed that this "present revolution" of southern secession was sure to spark a future revolution of freedom for the slaves. Garfield quoted with approval William H. Seward's Irrepressible Conflict speech predicting a showdown between the slave South and the free-labor North. Garfield echoed Seward's certainty of the outcome. The rise of the Republican party, they agreed, was a "revolution," and "revolutions never go backward." If civil war followed from secession, wrote Garfield, so be it, for the Bible taught that "without the shedding of blood there is no remission of sins." Or as Hinsdale put it: "All the great charters of humanity have been writ in blood. . . . England's was engrossed in that [the blood] of the Stuarts—and that of the United States in [the blood] of England." Soon, perhaps, the slaves would achieve their charter of freedom in the blood of their masters.[1]

When the war came, Garfield joined the Union army and rose eventually to the rank of major general. For him the war was, quite literally, the second American Revolution. In

October 1862, he insisted that the conflict of arms must destroy "the old slaveholding, aristocratic social dynasty" that had ruled the nation, and replace it with a "new Republican one." A few months later, while reading Louis Adolphe Thiers's ten-volume *History of the French Revolution*, Garfield was "constantly struck" with "the remarkable analogy which the events of that day bear to our own rebellious times."[2]

In December 1863, Garfield doffed his army uniform for the civilian garb of a congressman. During the first three of his seventeen years in Congress, he was one of the most radical of the radical Republicans. In his maiden speech to the House on January 28, 1864, Garfield called for the confiscation of the land of Confederate planters and its redistribution among freed slaves and white Unionists in the South. To illustrate the need for such action, he drew upon the experience of the English revolution against the Stuarts and the American Revolution against Britain. "Our situation," said Garfield, "affords a singular parallel to that of the people of Great Britain in their great revolution" and an even more important parallel to our forefathers of 1776. "Every one of the thirteen States, with a single exception, confiscated the real and personal property of Tories in arms." The southern planters were the Tories of this second American Revolution, he continued, and to break their power we must not only emancipate their slaves, "we must [also] take away the platform on which slavery stands—the great landed estates of the armed rebels. . . . Take that land away, and divide it into homes for the men who have saved our country." And after their land was taken away, Garfield went on, "the leaders of this rebellion must be executed or banished. . . . They must follow the fate of the Tories of the Revolution." These were harsh measures, Garfield admitted, but "let no weak sentiments of misplaced sympathy deter us from inaugurating a measure which will

cleanse our nation and make it the fit home of freedom. . . .
Let us not despise the severe wisdom of our Revolutionary
fathers when they served their generation in a similar way."[3]

Garfield later receded from his commitment to confiscation and his belief in execution or banishment. But he continued to insist on the enfranchisement of freed slaves as
voters, a measure that many contemporaries viewed as revolutionary. He linked this also to the ideas of the first American Revolution. The Declaration of Independence, said
Garfield in a speech on July 4, 1865, proclaimed the equal
birthright of all men and the need for the consent of the
governed for a just government. This meant black men as
well as white men, he said, and to exclude emancipated
slaves from equal participation in government would be a
denial of "the very axioms of the Declaration."[4]

In 1866, Congress passed the Fourteenth Amendment to
the Constitution as a compromise that granted blacks equal
civil rights but not equal voting rights. When the southern
states nevertheless refused to ratify this moderate measure,
Garfield renewed his call for revolutionary change to be
imposed on the South by its northern conquerors. Since
southern whites, he said in early 1867, "would not co-oper-
ate with us in rebuilding what they had destroyed, we must
remove the rubbish and rebuild from the bottom. . . . We
must lay the heavy hand of military authority upon these
Rebel communities, and . . . plant liberty on the ruins of
slavery."[5]

This rhetoric of revolution was hardly unique to Garfield.
Numerous abolitionists, radical Republicans, and radical
army officers were saying the same things. The abolitionist
Wendell Phillips was the most articulate spokesman for a
revolutionary policy. He insisted that the Civil War "is primarily a social revolution. . . . The war can ony be ended
by annihilating that Oligarchy which formed and rules the
South and makes the war—by annihilating a state of so-

ciety. . . . The whole social system of the Gulf States must be taken to pieces." The congressional leader of the radical Republicans, Thaddeus Stevens, was equally outspoken. We must "treat this war as a radical revolution," he said. Reconstruction must "revolutionize Southern institutions, habits, and manners. . . . The foundations of their institutions . . . must be broken up and relaid, or all our blood and treasure have been spent in vain." The colonel of a Massachusetts regiment stationed in the occupied portion of South Carolina during 1862 said that the war could be won and peace made permanent only by "changing, revolutionizing, absorbing the institutions, life, and manners of the conquered people."[6]

European radicals also viewed the American Civil War as a revolution. In London, Karl Marx followed the American war with intense interest. He wrote about it in articles for a Vienna newspaper and in private letters to his colleague Friedrich Engels. Marx described the war for the Union against the "slave oligarchy" as a potentially "world transforming . . . revolutionary movement" if the North would only seize the moment to proclaim the abolition of slavery. When Lincoln did so, Marx was ecstatic. "Never has such a gigantic transformation taken place so rapidly" as the liberation of four million slaves. "Out of the death of slavery" would spring "a new and vigorous life" for working-class people of all races, wrote Marx, for "labor with a white skin cannot emancipate itself where labor with a black skin is branded. . . . Workingmen of Europe feel sure that as the American War of Independence initiated a new era of ascendancy for the middle class, so the American Antislavery War will do for the working classes."[7] Georges Clemenceau of France, future leader of the French Left and premier of France in the later stages of World War I, was the American correspondent of a radical French newspaper from 1866 to 1869. In articles written from Washington, where Clemenceau came particularly to admire Thaddeus Stevens, the young French journalist described the abolition of slavery and enfranchisement of the freedmen as "one of the most radical revolutions known in history." A British writer chimed in with a description of Stevens as "the Robespierre, Danton, and Marat of America, all rolled into one."[8]

Hostile contemporaries concurred with this appraisal of the Civil War's revolutionary impact. The conservative and pro-Confederate *Times* of London described the radical Republicans as the Jacobins of the second American Revolution, a label picked up by subsequent historians who used it as an epithet to portray the radicals as bloodthirsty fanatics. A Democratic newspaper in Boston likewise compared radicals to "the 'Committee of Twelve' of the days of the Reign of Terror." A few weeks after Appomattox the *New York Herald,* notorious during the war for its hostility to Republican war policies including emancipation, concluded that by destroying both slavery and "the domineering slaveholding aristocracy . . . this tremendous war has wrought in four years the revolutionary changes which would probably have required a hundred years of peace."[9] An anguished editor in Memphis declared in 1865 that "the events of the last five years have produced an entire revolution in the entire Southern country." And two years later a South Carolina journalist, reacting to the enfranchisement of the freedmen, pronounced it "the maddest, most infamous revolution in history."[10]

Among historians the notion of the Civil War as the second American Revolution is identified most closely with Charles A. Beard. But in Beard's view, slavery and emancipation were almost incidental to the real causes and consequences of the war. The sectional conflict arose from the contending economic interests of plantation agriculture and industrializing capitalism. Slavery happened to be the labor system of plantation agriculture, Beard conceded, but apart from that it was not a crucial issue in and of itself except for a handful of abolitionists. In effect, the war was a class conflict between a Yankee capitalist bourgeoisie and a southern planter aristocracy. "Merely by the accidents of climate, soil, and geography," wrote Beard, "was it a sectional struggle." The triumph of the North under the leadership of the Republican party, which represented the interests of northern capitalism, brought about "the unquestioned establishment of a new power in the government, making vast changes in the arrangement of classes, in the distribution of wealth, in the course of industrial development." If the overthrow of the king and the aristocracy by the middle classes of England in the 1640s was to be known as the Puritan Revolution, and the overthrow of king, nobility, and clergy by the middle classes and peasants of France as the French Revolution, maintained Beard, then "the social cataclysm in which the capitalists, laborers, and farmers of the North and West drove from power in the national government the planting aristocracy of the South" was the "Second American Revolution, and in a strict sense, the First"—the first because the Revolution of 1776 had produced no such changes in the distribution of wealth and power among classes.[11]

Beard's interpretation was a modern variant of Marx's perception of the Civil War, with the question of slavery—which was of central importance for Marx—shunted into the wings. Although not strictly a Marxist, Beard was influenced by reading Marx. Avowed Marxian historians such as Herbert Aptheker and James S. Allen (the pen name of Sol Auerbach) have emphasized more than did Beard the issue of slavery. For them, the outcome of the Civil War was not merely a triumph of northern industrial capitalism over plantation agriculture; it was also a victory of the radical bourgeoisie in alliance with the black proletariat and elements of the white proletariat over the southern aristocracy.[12] That a large percentage of the white "proletariat" in both North and South either supported the Confederacy or opposed emancipation, however, is something of an embarrassment to the Marxian interpretation.

A scholar whose work owes much to Marxian analytical categories is Barrington Moore, who has portrayed the Civil War as "the last Capitalist Revolution." Moore's argument is subtle and complex, hard to summarize briefly without distortion. He sees the revolutionary dimension of the war not simply as a triumph of freedom over slavery, or industrialism over agriculture, or the bourgeoisie over the plantation gentry—but as a combination of all these things. Plantation agriculture in the South was not a form of feudalism, Moore insists; rather, it was a special form of capitalism that spawned a value system and an ideology that glorified hereditary privilege, racial caste, and slavery while it rejected bourgeois conceptions of equality of opportunity, free labor, and social mobility. Thus the war was a struggle between two conflicting capitalist systems—one reactionary, based on slave labor, and fearful of change; the other progressive, competitive, innovative, and democratic. Although the slave system presented no obstacle to the growth of industrial capitalism as an *economic* system (here is where Moore differs from Beard), it did present a "formidable obstacle to the establishment of industrial capitalist democracy . . . at least any conception of democracy that includes the goals of human equality, even the limited form of equality of opportunity, and human freedom. . . . Labor-repressive agricultural systems, and plantation slavery in particular, are political obstacles to a *particular kind* of capitalism, at a specific historical stage: competitive democratic capitalism we must call it for lack of a more precise term." In this sense the free-labor ideology of the Republican party in the Civil War era was heir to the radical bourgeois ideologies of the English and French Revolutions; the triumph of this ideology in the 1860s was therefore the "last revolutionary offensive on the part of what one may legitimately call urban or bourgeois capitalist democracy. . . . It was a violent breakthrough against an older social structure."[13]

The number of historians as well as contemporaries who have perceived the Civil War as a revolutionary experience would seem to have established something of a consensus on this question. But in the 1960s and 1970s several historians questioned the idea that the Civil War accomplished any sort of genuine revolution, and some even denied that it produced much significant change in the social and economic structure of the South or in the status of black people.

The initial challenge to Beard's thesis of the war as an economic revolution came from economic historians in the 1960s. They argued, first, that the basic developments which produced the industrial revolution in the United States—the railroad, the corporation, the factory system, the techniques of mass production of interchangeable parts, the mechanization of agriculture, and many other aspects of a modernizing industrial economy—began a generation or more before the Civil War, and that while the war may have confirmed and accelerated some of these developments, it produced no fundamental change of direction. Economic historians demonstrated, second, that the decade of the 1860s experienced an actual slowing of the rate of economic growth, and therefore the war may have retarded rather than promoted industrialization.[14]

The first of these arguments is well taken. Crucial innovations in transportation, technology, agriculture, the organization of manufacturing, capital formation, and investment did take place in the first half of the nineteenth century. The Civil War did not begin the modernization and industrialization of the American economy. But this truth actually supports rather than contravenes the Beard and Moore theses. Most of these antebellum modernizing developments were concentrated in the North. The South remained a labor-intensive, labor-repressive undiversified agricultural economy. The contrasting economic systems of the antebellum North and South helped to generate the conflicting proslavery and antislavery ideologies that eventually led to war. Northern victory in the war was therefore a triumph for the northern economic system and the social values it had generated. The war discredited the economic ideology and destroyed the national political power of the planter class. In this sense, then, the Civil War produced a massive shift toward national domination by the northern model of competitive democratic free-labor capitalism, a transformation of revolutionary proportions as described by Beard and Moore.

This ties in with the second point concerning the slowdown in the rate of economic growth in the 1860s. It is true that growth during the decade which included the war was lower than in any other decade between the 1830s and 1930s. But these growth data include the South. The war accomplished a wholesale devastation of southern economic resources. If we consider the northern states alone, the stimulus of war production probably caused a spurt in the economic growth rate. It was the destruction of the southern economy that caused the lag. After the war the national economy grew at the fastest rate of the century for a couple of decades, a growth that represented a catching-up process from the lag of the 1860s caused by the war's impact on the South.

Let us take a closer look at that impact. Union invasion of the Confederacy and the destruction of southern war industries and transportation facilities, the abolition of slavery, the wastage of southern livestock, and the killing of one-quarter of the South's white male population of military age made an economic desert of large areas of the South. While the total value of northern wealth increased by 50 percent during the 1860s, southern wealth *decreased* by at least 60 percent. In 1860 the South's share of national wealth was 30 percent; in 1870 it was only 12 percent. In 1860 the average per capita income of southerners, including slaves, was two-thirds of the northern average; after the war the southern average dropped to less than two-fifths of the northern, and did not rise above that level for the rest of the nineteenth century.[15]

The withdrawal of southern representatives and senators from Congress when their states seceded also made possible the passage of Republican-sponsored legislation to promote certain kinds of economic development. For years the southern-dominated Democratic party had blocked these measures. But Congress during the war enacted higher tariffs to foster industrial development; national banking acts to restore part of the centralized banking system destroyed in the 1830s by Jacksonian Democrats; land grants and government loans to build the first transcontinental railroad; a homestead act to grant 160 acres of government land to settlers; and the land-grant college act of 1862, which turned over federal land to the states to provide income for the establishment of state agricultural and vocational colleges, which became the basis of the modern land-grant universities.[16]

The war had a crucial impact on the long-term sectional balance of power in the nation. Before 1861 the slave states, despite their declining percentage of the population, had used their domination first of the Jeffersonian Republican party and then the Jacksonian Democratic party to achieve an extraordinary degree of power in the national government. In 1861 the United States had lived under the Constitution for seventy-two years. During forty-nine of those years the president had been a southerner—and a slaveholder. After the Civil War a century passed before another resident of the South was elected president. In Congress, twenty-three of the thirty-six speakers of the House down to 1861, and twenty-four of the thirty-six presidents pro tem of the Senate, were from the South. For half a century after the war, *none* of the speakers or presidents pro tem was from the South. From 1789 to 1861, twenty of the thirty-five Supreme Court justices had been southerners. At all times during those years the South had a majority on the Court. But only five of the twenty-six justices appointed during the next half-century were southerners.

These sweeping transformations in the balance of economic and political power between North and South undoubtedly merit the label of revolution. But this was a revolution in an *external* sense. It was only part of what contemporaries meant when they described the war as a revolution. More important, in the eyes of many, was the *internal* revolution: the emancipation of four million slaves, their elevation to civil and political equality with whites, and the destruction of the old ruling class in the South—all within the space of a half-dozen years. This was what the disgruntled South Carolinian quoted earlier meant when he deplored Reconstruction as "the maddest, most infamous revolution in history." It was what Georges Clemenceau meant when he spoke of "one of the most radical revolutions known to history." This was what freed slaves meant in the 1860s when they said jubilantly, "the bottom rail's on top."

But during the later 1960s and 1970s—in the climate of disillusionment produced by the Vietnam War and the aftermath of the civil rights movement—a number of skeptical historians maintained that the bottom rail never was on top and that a true internal social revolution never took place.

Some argued that the Republican party's commitment to equal rights for freed slaves was superficial, flawed by racism, only partly implemented, and quickly abandoned.[17] Other historians maintained that the policies of the Union occupation army, the Freedmen's Bureau, and the national government operated in the interests of the white landowners rather than the black freedmen, and that they were designed to preserve a docile, dependent, cheap labor force in the South rather than to encourage a revolutionary transformation of land tenure and economic status.[18] And finally, another group of scholars asserted that the domination of the southern economy by the old planter class continued unbroken after the Civil War. By such devices as the crop lien system, debt peonage, sharecropping, and a host of legal restrictions on black labor mobility, the planters kept their labor force subservient and poor in a manner little different from slavery.[19] Thus, in the words of historian Louis Gerteis, the war and Reconstruction produced no "fundamental changes" in the "antebellum forms of economic and social organization in the South." No "social revolution" took place because the abolition of slavery produced no "specific changes either in the status of the former slaves or in the conditions under which they labored."[20]

These studies left the question of the Civil War's revolutionary dimensions in considerable doubt and confusion. Part of the problem stemmed from the elastic meaning of the word "revolution." The term is often thrown around with careless abandon. The concept has almost become trivialized. In our own time we have lived through the technological revolution, the cybernetic revolution, the sexual revolution, the black revolution, the green revolution, the feminist revolution, the youth revolution, the paperback revolution, and the revolution of rising expectations—to name but a few.

By such standards the Civil War was indeed a revolution—

but so was just about everything else in American history. If we turn for help to the large scholarly literature on revolutions, we find almost as wide a variety of meanings as in common parlance. Definitions range from such brief statements as: Revolution "connotes a sudden and far reaching change, a major break in the continuity of development"; or "a sudden overthrow of established authority, aimed at a fundamental change in the existing social order"; to more complex and sweeping definitions, such as "a Revolution is a rapid, fundamental, and violent domestic change in the dominant values and myths of a society, in its political institutions, social structure, leadership, and government activity and policies." Some analysts, mainly political scientists and political historians, focus on revolutions that overthrow existing governments. For one such analyst, revolution is a "sudden and violent change in the political system and government of a state," while another defines it as "the drastic, sudden substitution of one group in charge of the running of a territorial political entity for another group." But for other scholars, especially but by no means exclusively those influenced by Marxist thought, even a violent overthrow of political institutions or rulers is not a genuine revolution unless, in Marx's words, it produces "a social transformation in which the power of the obsolescent class is overthrown, and that of the progressive, revolutionary class is established in its place."[21]

Faced with such a bewildering variety of definitions, one is tempted to agree with the French historian who decided that the only way to study revolutions was to "accept as revolution what men of a certain period experienced as revolution and so named it themselves."[22] But since many contemporaries called the American Civil War a revolution, that would not help us with the analytical problem raised by historians who deny that it really *was* a revolution. Let us instead adopt a common-sense working definition of revolution, and then return to the question whether the Civil War meets this definition. Let us define revolution simply as the overthrow of the existing social and political order by internal violence. Does the Civil War qualify? Certainly it does on the grounds of violence. It was by far the most violent event in American history. The 620,000 soldiers killed in the Civil War almost equals the number of American fighting men killed in all the country's other wars combined. What about the overthrow of the existing social and political order? As noted earlier, in an external sense the war did destroy the South's national political power, so thoroughly crippled the region's economy that it took nearly a century to recover, and by abolishing slavery undermined the basis of the antebellum social order. In these respects, the Civil War overthrew the *ancien régime* about as thoroughly as any previous revolution in history had done.

But we must still confront the arguments that the war and Reconstruction did not accomplish a genuine revolution in race relations or labor relations in the South. To a considerable degree, these arguments are flawed by presentism, by a tendency to read history backwards, measuring change over time from the point of arrival rather than the point of departure. Such a viewpoint looks first at the disabilities and discrimination suffered by black Americans in the twentieth century and concludes that there must have been little or no change since slavery. But this is the wrong way to measure change. It is like looking through the wrong end of a telescope—everything appears smaller than it really is.

A few statistics will illustrate the point. When slavery was abolished, about 90 percent of the black population was illiterate. By 1880 the rate of black illiteracy had been reduced to 70 percent, and by 1900 to less than 50 percent. From the perspective of today, this may seem like minimal progress. The illiteracy of almost half the black population in 1900, compared with less than a tenth of the white population, may seem shameful. But viewed from the standpoint of 1865 the rate of literacy for blacks increased by 200 percent in fifteen years and by 400 percent in thirty-five years. This was significant change. Or take another set of educational data: in 1860 only 2 percent of the black children of school age in the United States were attending school. By 1880 this had increased to 34 percent. During the same period the proportion of white children of school age attending school had grown only from 60 to 62 percent. From one viewpoint, the proportion of black school attendance was still only half the proportion of white in 1880. But the change since 1860 was dramatic—indeed, revolutionary. The relative proportions of blacks and whites attending school had jumped from one-thirtieth to more than one-half. No other period of American history witnessed anything like so great a rate of relative change.[23]

Or let us look at the economic condition of the freed slaves in the generation after emancipation. This is the issue that has attracted most of the attention of historians who deny the existence of meaningful change. The grim reality of sharecropping and rural poverty in the South seems at first glance to confirm their argument. But studies of the economic consequences of emancipation by Roger Ransom and Richard Sutch provide evidence for a different conclusion. In the first place, Ransom and Sutch point out, the abolition of slavery represented a confiscation of about three billion dollars of property—the equivalent as a proportion of national wealth to at least three *trillion* dollars in 1990. In effect, the government in 1865 confiscated the principal form of property in one-third of the country, without compensation. That was without parallel in American history—it dwarfed the confiscation of Tory property in the American Revolution. When such a massive confiscation of property takes place as a consequence of violent internal upheaval on the scale of the American Civil War, it is quite properly called revolutionary.

The slaves constituted what economists call "human capital." Emancipation transferred the ownership of this capital to the freed slaves themselves. This had important consequences for the new owners of the capital, according to Ransom and Sutch. They calculate that under slavery, the slaves in the seven cotton states of the lower South had received in the form of food, clothing, and shelter only 22 percent of the income produced by the plantations and farms on which they worked. With the coming of freedom, this proportion jumped to 56 percent, owing to the ability of free laborers to bargain for higher wages—in the form of money or a share of the crop—than they had received as slaves. This did not mean that the overall standard of living improved quite so dramatically for blacks, because the postwar poverty of the southern agricultural economy meant that the average per capita income in the region declined. Blacks were getting a bigger share of the pie, but it was a smaller pie. Nevertheless, Ransom and Sutch conclude that between 1857 and 1879 the average per capita income for blacks in southern agriculture increased by 46 percent, while the per capita income of whites declined by about 35 percent. Put another way, black per capita income in these seven states jumped from a relative level of only 23 percent of white income under slavery to 52 percent of the white level by 1880. Thus, while blacks still had a standard of living only half as high as whites in the poorest region of the country—the negative point emphasized by the historians cited earlier—this relative redistribution of income within the South was by far the greatest in American history.[24]

Or consider the question of land ownership, a vital measure of wealth and status in an agricultural society. Again, at first glance the picture seems to confirm the argument of the "no change" historians. Abolitionists and Republicans like Garfield had urged the confiscation of land owned by wealthy Confederates and the allocation of part of this land to freed slaves. This would have been a truly revolutionary act. But confiscation was too radical for most Republicans, and even if they had tried it the Supreme Court might have ruled it unconstitutional. There was no meaningful land reform in the South. Planters lost their slaves but not their land. In this respect the war accomplished only half a revolution. Nevertheless, there were significant changes even in the matter of land ownership. In 1865 few blacks owned land in the South. But by 1880, 20 percent of the black farm operators owned part or all of the land they farmed (the rest were renters or sharecroppers). By 1910, 25 percent of the black farmers owned land. At the same time the proportion of white farmers who owned land was decreasing from more than 80 percent at the end of the war to 60 percent in 1910. Here again, while blacks remained far below whites, the war made possible a large and important relative change.[25]

Finally, let us look at one more index of change within the South—political power. At the beginning of 1867 no black man could vote in the South. A year later, blacks were a majority of registered voters in several ex-Confederate states. No black man yet held political office. But three or four years later, about 15 percent of the officeholders in the South were black—a larger proportion than in 1990. In 1870, blacks provided three-fourths of the votes in the South for the Republican party, which controlled the governments of a dozen states in which five years earlier most of these black voters had been slaves. It was this phenomenon, more than anything else, that caused contemporaries to describe the events of those years as a revolution.

It has also caused the historiographical pendulum in the 1980s to swing back toward a perception of the Civil

War and Reconstruction as a revolutionary experience. Two books by Eric Foner have been instrumental in this process. Foner points out that the United States was unique among post-emancipation societies in granting freed slaves equal political rights. This revolutionary act had important consequences for social and economic relations in the new order. "The Second American Revolution," writes Foner, "profoundly if temporarily affected the relationship of the state to the economic order. . . . The freedmen won, in the vote, a form of leverage their counterparts in other societies did not possess. . . . Radical Reconstruction stands as a unique moment when . . . political authority actually sought to advance the interests of the black laborer." As a South Carolina planter complained in 1872, "under the laws of most of the Southern States ample protection is afforded to tenants and very little to landlords."[26]

In Foner's judgment, this exercise of political power was more important than land redistribution would have been. The experience of freed slaves and of non-white peoples in the Caribbean, Africa, and other regions demonstrates that nominal ownership of land does little to foster economic independence "where political power rests with classes that are at worst hostile and at best indifferent to the fate of the rural population."[27] Reconstruction legislatures enacted certain taxes, mechanic's and renter's lien laws, measures concerning credit and the like that protected the interests of sharecroppers and wage-earners against landlords and employers. The "Redeemer" governments that overthrew Reconstruction in the 1870s reversed the relationship. A few examples will illustrate the point. In 1865–66 southern state governments had adopted "Black Codes" to keep black labor in a state of dependence and subjection as close to slavery as possible. The Freedmen's Bureau and federal courts suspended these codes; Republican state governments repealed them during Reconstruction; Redeemer governments in effect restored some of them in the form of landlord's liens, vagrancy laws, contract labor laws that amounted to peonage, anti-enticement laws to limit labor mobility, criminal statutes rigged against blacks, and a pattern of law enforcement that favored white over black and landlord over cropper. During Reconstruction the state of South Carolina set up a land commission that sold land to 14,000 black families on easy terms; the Redeemer government retained the commission but changed its administration in such a way as to foreclose on the properties of most of these families and transfer the land to white ownership. When Republicans controlled the South Carolina government, black rice workers struck for higher wages in 1876 and won; across the Savannah River in Georgia, where Democrats ruled, wages on the rice plantations averaged less than half the level in South Carolina.[28]

In 1868 a black speaker at a political meeting in Savannah declared that "a revolution gave us the right to vote, and it will take a revolution to get it away from us."[29] That, unfortunately, is what happened. For freed slaves the second American Revolution turned out, in Foner's words, to be "America's unfinished revolution" because many of its gains were reversed by what Vice-President Henry Wilson described in 1874 as "a Counter-Revolution."[30] The Civil War *did* partially overthrow the existing social and political order in the South—overthrow it at least as much as did the English Revolution of the 1640s or the French Revolution of the 1790s. Neither of those revolutions totally destroyed the *ancien régime,* and both were followed by counterrevolutions that restored part of the old order, including the monarchy. But scarcely anyone denies the label revolution to those events in English and French history. The events of the 1860s in the United States equally deserve the label revolution. It also was followed by a counterrevolution, which combined white violence in the South with a revival of the Democratic party in the North and a growing indifference of northern Republicans toward the plight of southern blacks. The counterrevolution overthrew the fledgling experiment in racial equality. But it did not fully restore the old order. Slavery was not reinstated. The Fourteenth and Fifteenth Amendments were not repealed. Blacks continued to own land and to go to school. The counterrevolution was not as successful as the revolution had been. The second American Revolution left a legacy of black educational and social institutions, a tradition of civil rights activism, and constitutional amendments that provided the legal framework for the second Reconstruction of the 1960s.

II

Abraham Lincoln and the Second American Revolution

The foremost Lincoln scholar of a generation ago, James G. Randall, considered the sixteenth president to be a conservative on the great issues facing the country, Union and slavery. If conservatism, wrote Randall, meant "caution, prudent adherence to tested values, avoidance of rashness, and reliance upon unhurried, peaceable evolution, [then] Lincoln was a conservative." His preferred solution of the slavery problem, Randall pointed out, was a program of gradual, compensated emancipation with the consent of the owners, stretching over a generation or more, with provision for the colonization abroad of emancipated slaves to minimize the potential for racial conflict and social disorder. In his own words, Lincoln said that he wanted to "stand on middle ground," avoid "dangerous extremes," and achieve his goals through "the spirit of compromise . . . [and] of mutual concession." In essence, concluded Randall, Lincoln believed in evolution rather than revolution, in "planting, cultivating, and harvesting, not in uprooting and destroying."[1] Many historians have agreed with this interpretation. To cite just two of them: T. Harry Williams maintained that "Lincoln was on the slavery question, as he was on most matters, a conservative"; and Norman Graebner wrote an essay entitled "Abraham Lincoln: Conservative

Statesman," based on the premise that Lincoln was a conservative because "he accepted the need of dealing with things as they were, not as he would have wished them to be."[2]

Yet as president of the United States, Lincoln presided over a profound, wrenching experience which, in Mark Twain's words, "uprooted institutions that were centuries old, changed the politics of a people, transformed the social life of half the country, and wrought so profoundly upon the entire national character that the influence cannot be measured short of two or three generations." Benjamin Disraeli, viewing this experience from across the Atlantic in 1863, characterized "the struggle in America" as "a great revolution. . . . [We] will see, when the waters have subsided, a different America."[3] The *Springfield* (Mass.) *Republican*, an influential wartime newspaper, predicted that Lincoln's Emancipation Proclamation would accomplish "the greatest social and political revolution of the age." The historian Otto Olsen has labeled Lincoln a revolutionary because he led the nation in its achievement of this result.[4]

As for Lincoln himself, he said repeatedly that the right of revolution, the "right of any people" to "throw off, to revolutionize, their existing form of government, and to establish such other in its stead as they may choose" was "a sacred right—a right, which we may hope and believe, is to liberate the world." The Declaration of Independence, he insisted often, was the great "charter of freedom" and in the example of the American Revolution "the world has found . . . the germ . . . to grow and expand into the universal liberty of mankind." Lincoln championed the leaders of the European revolutions of 1848; in turn, a man who knew something about those revolutions—Karl Marx—praised Lincoln in 1865 as "the single-minded son of the working class" who had led his "country through the matchless struggle for the rescue of an enchained race and the reconstruction of a social world."[5]

What are we to make of these contrasting portraits of Lincoln the conservative and Lincoln the revolutionary? Are they just another example of how Lincoln's words can be manipulated to support any position, even diametrically opposed ones? No. It is a matter of interpretation and emphasis within the context of a fluid and rapidly changing crisis situation. The Civil War started out as one kind of conflict and ended as something quite different. These apparently contradictory positions about Lincoln the conservative versus Lincoln the revolutionary can be reconciled by focusing on this process. The attempt to reconcile them can tell us a great deal about the nature of the American Civil War.

That war has been viewed as a revolution—as the second American Revolution—in three different senses. Lincoln played a crucial role in defining the outcome of the revolution in each of three respects.

The first way in which some contemporaries regarded the events of 1861 as a revolution was the frequent invocation of the right of revolution by southern leaders to justify their secession—their declaration of independence—from the United States. The Mississippi convention that voted to secede in 1861 listed the state's grievances against the North, and proclaimed: "For far less cause than this, our fathers separated from the Crown of England." The governor of Tennessee agreed that unless the North made concessions to the South, "the only alternative left to us [will be] to follow the example of our fathers of 1776." And an Alabama newspaper asked rhetorically: Were not "the men of 1776, who withdrew their allegiance from George III and set up for themselves . . . Secessionists?"[6]

Southerners created the Confederacy to protect their

"rights" against a perceived northern threat to those rights. If we remain in the Union, said a Virginia slaveholder, "we will be deprived of that right for which our fathers fought in the battles of the revolution." From "the high and solemn motive of defending and protecting the rights . . . which our fathers bequeathed to us," declared Jefferson Davis, let us "renew such sacrifices as our fathers made to the holy cause of constitutional liberty."[7] In the middle of the war, a Confederate army officer declared that he had "never believed the Constitution recognized the right of secession. I took up arms, sir, upon a broader ground—the right of revolution. We were wronged. Our properties and liberties were about to be taken from us. It was a sacred duty to rebel." A Confederate songster contained a stirring tune that linked the two revolutions, titled "Seventy-Six and Sixty-One." Another song contained the following words:

> *Rebels* before,
> Our fathers of yore,
> *Rebel*'s the righteous name
> *Washington* bore.
> Why, then, be ours the same.[8]

Northerners were unimpressed by these claims of revolutionary legitimacy. The principal right and liberty that southerners feared would be threatened if they remained in a Union governed by "Black Republicans" was their right to own slaves and their liberty to take them where they pleased in territories of the United States. "Will you consent to be robbed of your property," secession leaders asked their fellow Mississippians, or will you "strike bravely for liberty, property, honor and life?" A Georgia secessionist declared dramatically that if the South stayed in a Union "ruled by Lincoln and his crew . . . in TEN years or less our children will be the *slaves* of negroes. For emancipation must follow and negro equality is the same result."[9] William Cullen Bryant, antislavery editor of the *New York Evening Post,* cited such statements to ridicule southern claims to be following in the footsteps of their revolutionary forebears. That "is a libel upon the whole character and conduct of the men of '76," said Bryant. The founders fought "to establish the rights of man . . . and principles of universal liberty." The South was rebelling "not in the interest of general humanity, but of a domestic despotism. . . . Their motto is not liberty, but slavery." Thomas Jefferson's Declaration of Independence, added the *New York Tribune,* invoked "Natural Rights against Established Institutions," while "Mr. Jeff. Davis's caricature thereof is made in the interest of an unjust, outgrown, decaying Institution against the apprehended encroachments of Natural Human Rights." It was, in short, not a revolution but rather a counterrevolution "reversing the wheels of progress . . . to hurl everything backward into deepest darkness . . . despotism and oppression."[10]

Many secessionists conceded that their movement was essentially a counterrevolution against the anticipated revolutionary threat to slavery. Indeed, they proudly affirmed it. "We are not revolutionists," insisted James B. D. DeBow, the South's leading journalist; "we are resisting revolution." It was "an abuse of language" to call secession a revolution, said Jefferson Davis. "Ours is not a revolution." We left the Union "to save ourselves from a revolution" that threatened to make "property in slaves so insecure as to be comparatively worthless. . . . Our struggle is for inherited rights."[11] The Black Republicans were the real revolutionaries, southerners insisted, "a motley throng of Sans culottes . . . Infidels and freelovers, interspersed by Bloomer women, fugitive slaves, and amalgamationists . . . active and bristling with terrible designs and as ready for bloody and forcible realities as ever characterized the ideas of the French revolution."[12] Secession was therefore a "political revolution," explained a Georgian in 1860, to forestall the "social revolution" sure to come if the South remained in the Union. In 1861 the Confederate secretary of state advised foreign governments that southern states had formed a new nation "to preserve their old institutions" from "a revolution [that] threatened to destroy their social system."[13]

Northerners could scarcely have denied to the South the right of revolution for just cause, since Yankees were as much heirs of the legacy of 1776 as southerners were. But that phrase, "for just cause," is crucial. "It may seem strange," said Lincoln of Confederate leaders, "that any men should dare to ask a just God's assistance in wringing their bread from the sweat of other men's faces." Secession was not a just revolution, but an unjust counterrevolution. As Lincoln phrased it in the summer of 1861, "the right of revolution, is never a legal right. . . . At most, it is but a moral right, when exercised for a morally justifiable cause. When exercised without such a cause revolution is no right, but simply a wicked exercise of physical power."[14]

In Lincoln's view, secession was just such a wicked exercise. The event that precipitated it was his own election, which had been achieved by a constitutional majority according to constitutional procedures. The Republicans had done nothing against the law, had violated nobody's constitutional rights. Indeed, seven states had seceded and formed the Confederacy a month before Lincoln even took office. As northerners saw it, the South, having controlled the national government for most of the previous two generations through its domination of the Democratic party, now decided to leave the Union just because it had lost an election.

For Lincoln it was the *Union,* not the Confederacy, that was the true heir of the Revolution of 1776. That revolution had established a republic, a democratic government of the people by the people. This republic was a fragile experiment in a world of kings, emperors, tyrants, and theories of aristocracy. If secession were allowed to succeed, it would destroy that experiment. It would set a fatal precedent by which the minority could secede whenever it did not like what the majority stood for, until the United States fragmented into a dozen pitiful, squabbling countries, the laughing stock of the world. The successful establishment of a slaveholding Confederacy would also enshrine the idea of inequality, a contradiction of the ideal of equal natural rights on which the United States was founded. "This issue embraces more than the fate of these United States," said Lincoln on another occasion. "It presents to the whole family of man, the question, whether a constitutional republic, or a democracy . . . can, or cannot, maintain its territorial integrity." Nor is the struggle "altogether for today; it is for a vast future. . . . On the side of the Union it is a struggle for maintaining in the world that form and substance of government whose leading object is to elevate the condition of men . . . to afford all an unfettered start, and a fair chance in the race of life."[15]

To *preserve* the Union and *maintain* the republic: these verbs denote a conservative purpose. If the Confederacy's war of independence was indeed a revolution, Lincoln was most certainly a conservative. But if secession was an act of counterrevolution to forestall a revolutionary threat to slavery posed by the government Lincoln headed, these verbs take on a different meaning and Lincoln's intent to conserve the Union becomes something other than conservatism. But precisely what it would become was not yet clear in 1861.

The second respect in which the Civil War is viewed as a revolution was in its abolition of slavery. This was indeed a revolutionary achievement—not only an expropriation of the principal form of property in half the country, but a destruction of the institution that was basic to the southern social order, the political structure, the culture, the way of life in this region. But in 1861 this revolutionary achievement was not part of Lincoln's war aims.

From the beginning of the war, though, abolitionists and some Republicans urged the Lincoln administration to turn the military conflict into a revolutionary crusade to abolish slavery and create a new order in the South. As one abolitionist put it in 1861, although the Confederates "justify themselves under the right of revolution," their cause "is not a revolution but a rebellion against the noblest of revolutions." The North must meet this southern counterrevolution by converting the war for the Union into a revolution for freedom. "WE ARE THE REVOLUTIONISTS," he proclaimed. The principal defect of the first American Revolution, in the eyes of abolitionists, had been that while it freed white Americans from British rule it failed to free black Americans from slavery. Now was the time to remedy that defect by proclaiming emancipation and inviting the slaves "to a share in the *glorious second American Revolution*." And Thaddeus Stevens, the grim-visaged old gladiator who led the radical Republicans in the House of Representatives, pulled no punches in this regard. "We must treat this [war] as a radical revolution," he declared, and "free every slave—slay every traitor—burn every rebel mansion, if these things be necessary to preserve" the nation.[16]

Such words grated harshly on Lincoln's ears during the first year of the war. In his message to Congress in December 1861 the president deplored the possibility that the war might "degenerate into a violent and remorseless revolutionary struggle." It was not that Lincoln *wanted* to preserve slavery. On the contrary, he said many times: "I am naturally anti-slavery. If slavery is not wrong, nothing is wrong." But as president he could not act officially on his private "judgment [concerning] the moral question of slavery." He was bound by the Constitution, which protected the institution of slavery in the states.[17] In the first year of the war the North fought to preserve this Constitution and restore the Union as it had existed before 1861. Lincoln's theory of the war held that since secession was illegal, the Confederate states were still legally in the Union although temporarily under the control of insurrectionists. The government's purpose was to suppress this insurrection and restore loyal Unionists to control of the southern states. The conflict was therefore a limited war with the limited goal of restoring the status quo ante bellum, not an unlimited war to destroy an enemy nation and reshape its society. And since, in theory, the southern states were still in the Union, they continued to enjoy all their constitutional rights, including slavery.

There were also several political reasons for Lincoln to take this conservative position in 1861. For one thing, the four border slave states of Missouri, Kentucky, Maryland, and Delaware had remained in the Union; Lincoln desperately wanted to keep them there. He would like to have God on his side, Lincoln supposedly said, but he *must* have Kentucky. In all of these four states except Delaware a strong pro-Confederate faction existed. Any rash action by the northern government against slavery, therefore, might push three more states into the Confederacy. Moreover, in the North itself nearly half of the voters were Democrats, who supported a war for the Union but might oppose a war against slavery. For these reasons, Lincoln held at bay the Republicans and abolitionists who were calling for an anti-slavery war and revoked actions by two of his generals who had proclaimed emancipation by martial law in areas under their command.

Antislavery Republicans challenged the theory underlying Lincoln's concept of a limited war. They pointed out that by 1862 the conflict had become in theory as well as in fact a full-fledged war between nations, not just a police action to suppress an uprising. By imposing a blockade on Confederate ports and treating captured Confederate soldiers as prisoners of war rather than as criminals or pirates, the Lincoln administration had in effect recognized that this was a war rather than a mere domestic insurrection. Under international law, belligerent powers had the right to seize or destroy enemy resources used to wage war—munitions, ships, military equipment, even food for the armies and crops sold to obtain cash to buy armaments. As the war escalated in scale and fury and as Union armies invaded the South in 1861, they did destroy or capture such resources. Willy-nilly the war *was* becoming a remorseless revolutionary conflict, a total war rather than a limited one.

A major Confederate resource for waging war was the slave population, which constituted a majority of the southern labor force. Slaves raised food for the army, worked in war industries, built fortifications, dug trenches, drove army supply wagons, and so on. As enemy property, these slaves were subject to confiscation under the laws of war. The Union Congress passed limited confiscation laws in August 1861 and July 1862 that authorized the seizure of this human property. But pressure mounted during 1862 to go further than this—to proclaim emancipation as a *means* of winning the war by converting the slaves from a vital war resource for the South to allies of the North, and beyond that to make the abolition of slavery a *goal* of the war, in order to destroy the institution that had caused the war in the first place and would continue to plague the nation in the future if it was allowed to survive. By the summer of 1861, most Republicans wanted to turn this limited war to restore the old Union into a revolutionary war to create a new nation purged of slavery.

For a time Lincoln tried to outflank this pressure by persuading the border slave states remaining in the Union to undertake voluntary, gradual emancipation, with the owners to be compensated by the federal government. With rather dubious reasoning, Lincoln predicted that such action would shorten the war by depriving the Confederacy of its hope for the allegiance of these states and thereby induce the South to give up the fight. And though the compensation of slaveholders would be expensive, it would cost much less than continuing the war. If the border states adopted some plan of gradual emancipation such as northern states had done after the Revolution of 1776, said Lincoln, the process would not radically disrupt the social order.

Three times in the spring and summer of 1862 Lincoln appealed to congressmen from the border states to endorse a plan for gradual emancipation. If they did not, he warned in March, "it is impossible to foresee all the incidents which may attend and all the ruin which may follow." In May he declared that the changes produced by his gradual plan "would come gently as the dews of heaven, not rending or wrecking anything. Will you not embrace it? . . . You can not, if you would, be blind to the signs of the times." But most of the border-state representatives remained blind to the signs. They questioned the constitutionality of Lincoln's proposal, objected to its cost, bristled at its veiled threat of federal coercion, and deplored the potential race problem they feared would come with a large free black population. In July, Lincoln once more called border-state congressmen to the White House. He admonished them bluntly that "the unprecedentedly stern facts of the case" called for immediate action. The limited war was becoming a total war; pressure to turn it into a war of abolition was growing. The slaves were emancipating themselves by running away from home and coming into Union lines. If the border states did not make "a decision at once to emancipate gradually . . . the institution in your states will be extinguished by mere friction and abrasion—by the mere incidents of the war." In other words, if they did not accept an evolutionary plan for the abolition of slavery, it would be wiped out by the revolution that was coming. But again they refused, rejecting Lincoln's proposal by a vote of twenty to nine. Angry and disillusioned, the president decided to embrace the revolution. That very evening he made up his mind to issue an emancipation proclamation. After a delay to wait for a Union victory, he sent forth the preliminary proclamation on September 22—after the battle of Antietam—and the final proclamation on New Year's Day 1863.[18]

The old cliché, that the proclamation did not free a single slave because it applied only to the Confederate states where Lincoln had no power, completely misses the point. The proclamation announced a revolutionary new war aim— the overthrow of slavery by force of arms if and when Union armies conquered the South. Of course, emancipation could not be irrevocably accomplished without a constitutional amendment, so Lincoln threw his weight behind the Thirteenth Amendment, which the House passed in January 1865. In the meantime two of the border states, Maryland and Missouri, which had refused to consider gradual, compensated emancipation in 1862, came under control of emancipationists who pushed through state constitutional amendments that abolished slavery without compensation and went into effect immediately—a fate experienced by the other border states, Kentucky and Delaware, along with the rest of the South when the Thirteenth Amendment was ratified in December 1865.

But from the time the Emancipation Proclamation went into effect at the beginning of 1863, the North fought for the revolutionary goal of a new Union without slavery. Despite grumbling and dissent by some soldiers who said they had enlisted to fight for the Union rather than for the "nigger," most soldiers understood and accepted the new policy. A colonel from Indiana put it this way: whatever their opinion of slavery and blacks, his men "desire to destroy everything that gives the rebels strength." Therefore "this army will sustain the emancipation proclamation and enforce it with the bayonet." Soon after the proclamation came out, General-in-Chief Henry W. Halleck wrote to General Ulysses S. Grant near Vicksburg that "the character of the war has very much changed within the last year. There is now no possible hope of reconciliation with the rebels. . . . We must conquer the rebels or be conquered by them. . . . Every slave withdrawn from the enemy is the equivalent of a white man put *hors de combat.*" One of Grant's field commanders explained that "the policy is to be terrible on the enemy. I am using negroes all the time for my work as teamsters, and have 1,000 employed."[19]

Lincoln endorsed this policy of being "terrible on the enemy." And the policy soon went beyond using freed slaves as teamsters and laborers. By early 1863 the Lincoln administration committed itself to enlisting black men in the army. Arms in the hands of slaves constituted the South's ultimate nightmare. The enlistment of black soldiers to fight and kill their former masters was by far the most revolutionary dimension of the emancipation policy. And, after overcoming his initial hesitation, Lincoln became an enthusiastic advocate of this policy. In March 1863 he wrote to Andrew Johnson, military governor of occupied Tennessee: "The bare sight of fifty thousand armed, and drilled black soldiers on the banks of the Mississippi, would end the rebellion at once. And who doubts that we can present that sight, if we but take hold in earnest?" By August 1863, when the Union army had organized 50,000 black soldiers and was on the way to enlistment of 180,000 before the war was over, Lincoln declared in a public letter that "the emancipation policy, and the use of colored troops, constitute the heaviest blow yet dealt to the rebellion."[20]

When conservatives complained of the revolutionary nature of these heavy blows, Lincoln responded that the nation could no longer pursue "a temporizing and forbearing" policy toward rebels. "Decisive and extensive measures must be adopted." Conservatives who did not like it should blame the slaveholders and fire-eaters who started the war. They "must understand," said Lincoln in an angry tone, "that they cannot experiment for ten years trying to destroy the government, and if they fail still come back into the Union unhurt." In a metaphor that he used several times, Lincoln said that "broken eggs cannot be mended." The egg of slavery was already broken by 1862; if the South continued fighting it must expect more eggs to be broken, so the sooner it gave up "the smaller [would] be the amount of that which will be beyond mending."[21] Lincoln's fondness for this metaphor is interesting, for modern revolutionaries sometimes use a similar one to justify the use of violence to bring about social change: you cannot make an omelet, they say, without breaking eggs—that is, you cannot make a new society without destroying the old one.

Another way of illustrating how Lincoln came to believe in this revolutionary concept is to quote from his second inaugural address, delivered at a time when the war had gone on for almost four terrible years. On the one hand were the famous words of the second inaugural calling for the binding up of the nation's wounds, with malice toward none and charity for all. With these words Lincoln invoked the New Testament lesson of forgiveness; he urged a soft peace once the war was over. But although he believed in a soft peace, it could be won only by a hard war. This was an Old Testament concept, and for Lincoln's Old Testament vision of a hard war, examine *this* passage from the second inaugural: "American Slavery is one of those offences which, in the providence of God . . . He now wills to remove [through] this terrible war, as the woe due to those by whom the offence came. . . . Fondly do we hope—fervently do we pray—that this mighty scourge of war may speedily pass away. Yet if God wills that it continue, until all the wealth piled by the bondman's two hundred and fifty years of unrequited toil shall be sunk, and until every drop of blood drawn with the lash, shall be paid by another drawn with the sword, as was said three thousand years ago, so still it must be said 'the judgments of the Lord, are true and righteous altogether.' "[22]

This was the language not only of the Old Testament, but also of revolution. In the second respect in which the Civil War has been viewed as a revolution—its achievement of the abolition of slavery—Lincoln fits the pattern of a revolutionary leader. He was a reluctant one at first, to be sure, but in the end he was more radical than Washington or Jefferson or any of the leaders of the first revolution. They led a successful struggle for independence from Britain but did not accomplish a fundamental change in the society they led. Lincoln did preside over such a change. Indeed, as he put it himself, also in the second inaugural, neither side had anticipated such "fundamental and astounding" changes when the war began.

These words introduce the third respect in which the Civil War can be viewed as a revolution: it destroyed not only slavery but also the social structure of the old South that had been founded on slavery, and it radically altered the power balance between the North and the South. It changed the direction of American development. This was what Mark Twain meant when he wrote that the war had "uprooted institutions that were centuries old . . . transformed the social life of half the country, and wrought so profoundly upon the entire national character." It was what Charles A. Beard meant when he wrote (as quoted in the preceding essay) that the Civil War was a "social cataclysm . . . making vast changes in the arrangement of classes, in the distribution of wealth, in the course of industrial development."

The war ended seventy years of southern domination of the national government and transferred it to Yankee Republicans who controlled the polity and economy of the United States for most of the next seventy years. It increased northern wealth and capital by 50 percent during the 1860s while destroying 60 percent of southern wealth. The output of southern industry in proportion to that of the North was cut in half by the war; the value of southern agricultural land in relation to that of the North was cut by three-fourths.

These changes occurred because when the Civil War became a total war, the invading army intentionally destroyed the economic capacity of the South to wage war. Union armies ripped up thousands of miles of southern railroads and blew up hundreds of bridges; Confederate cavalry raids and guerrilla operations behind Union lines in the South added to the destruction. More than half of the South's farm machinery was wrecked by the war, two-fifths of its livestock was killed, and one-quarter of its white males of military age—also the prime age for economic production—were killed, a higher proportion than suffered by any European power in World War I, that holocaust which ravaged a continent and spread revolution through many of its countries.

Union generals William Tecumseh Sherman and Philip Sheridan saw more clearly than anyone else the nature of modern total war, a war between peoples rather than simply between armies, a war in which the fighting left nothing untouched or unchanged. "We are not only fighting hostile armies, but a hostile people," wrote Sherman in the middle of the war. "We cannot change the hearts of those people of the South," he said in 1864 as his army began its march from Atlanta to the sea, "but we can make war so terrible . . . that generations would pass away before they would again appeal to it."[23] While Sherman's army was marching through Georgia and South Carolina destroying everything in its path, Sheridan's army cut a similar swath through the Shenandoah Valley making sure that it, like Georgia and South Carolina, would produce no more food or munitions for Confederate forces.

Although Abraham Lincoln was a compassionate man who deplored this destruction and suffering, he nevertheless assented to it as the only way to win the war. After all, he had warned southerners two years earlier that the longer they fought, the more eggs would be broken. Now, in 1864, he officially conveyed to Sheridan the "thanks of the nation, and my own personal admiration and gratitude, for [your] operations in the Shenandoah Valley"; he sent Sherman and his army "grateful acknowledgments" for their march through Georgia.[24]

The second American Revolution, as Charles Beard viewed it, involved not only this destruction of the southern plantation gentry but also the consolidation of the northern entrepreneurial capitalist class in national power, supported by its rural and urban middle-class allies. Legislation passed by the Union Congress during the war promoted this development. The Republican party had inherited from its Hamiltonian and Whig forebears a commitment to the use of government to foster economic development through tariffs to protect industry, a centralized and regulated banking system, investment subsidies and land grants to high-risk but socially beneficial transportation enterprises, and government support for education. By 1860 the Republican party had also pledged itself to homestead legislation to provide farmers with an infusion of capital in the form of free land. Before 1860, the southern-dominated Democratic party that controlled the federal government had repeatedly defeated or frustrated these measures. During the war, Republicans passed them all: a higher tariff in 1861; a homestead act, a land-grant college act, and a Pacific railroad act providing loans and land grants for a transcontinental railroad in 1862; and a national banking act in 1863, which, along with the legal tender act of the previous year authorizing the issuance of a federal currency, the famous greenbacks, gave the national government effective control over the nation's currency for the first time. In addition, to finance the war the government marketed huge bond issues to the public and passed an Internal Revenue Act which imposed a large array of federal taxes for the first time, including a progressive income tax.

This astonishing blitz of laws, most of them passed within the span of less than one year, did more to reshape the relation of the government to the economy than any comparable effort except perhaps the first hundred days of the New Deal. This Civil War legislation, in the words of one historian, created a "blueprint for modern America." It helped promote what another scholar termed "the last capitalist revolution" whereby the Civil War destroyed the "older social structure of plantation slavery" and installed "competitive democratic capitalism" in unchallenged domination of the American economy and polity. That this capitalism itself became a form of entrenched conservatism exploiting labor and resisting change a generation or two later does not nullify the revolutionary meaning of its triumph over the slave South and plantation agriculture in the 1860s. And as a former Whig who had favored these measures to promote banking, transportation, and industry as a means of bringing a higher standard of living to all Americans, and who believed that the abolition of slave labor would enhance the dignity and value of free labor, Agraham Lincoln was one of the principal architects of this capitalist revolution.[25]

What conclusions can we draw, then, that make sense of those contrasting pictures of Lincoln the conservative and Lincoln the revolutionary quoted at the beginning of this essay? Although it may seem like an oxymoron, Lincoln can best be described as a conservative revolutionary. That is, he wanted to conserve the Union as the revolutionary heritage of the founding fathers. Preserving this heritage was the *purpose* of the war; all else became a means to achieve this end. As Lincoln phrased it in his famous public letter to Horace Greeley in August 1862, "My paramount object in this struggle *is* to save the Union, and is *not* either to save or to destroy slavery. . . . What I do about slavery and the colored race, I do because I believe it helps to save the Union."[26] By the time he wrote these words, Lincoln had made up his mind that to save the Union he must destroy slavery. The means always remained subordinated to the end, but the means did become as essential to the northern war effort as the end itself. In that sense perhaps we could describe Lincoln as a pragmatic revolutionary, for as a pragmatist he adapted the means to the end. Thus we can agree with the historian Norman Graebner who was quoted earlier as stating that Lincoln "accepted the need of dealing with things as they were, not as he would have wished them to be." But instead of concluding, as Graebner did, that this made Lincoln a conservative, we must conclude that it made him a revolutionary. Not an ideological revolutionary, to be sure—Lincoln was no Robespierre or Lenin with a blueprint for a new order—but he was a pragmatic revolutionary who found it necessary to destroy slavery and create a new birth of freedom in order to preserve the Union.

"The dogmas of the quiet past," Lincoln told Congress in December 1862, "are inadequate to the stormy present. As our case is new, we must think anew, and act anew." It was *the war itself,* not the ideological blueprints of Lincoln or any other leader, that generated the radical momentum that made it a second American revolution. Like most wars that become total wars, the Civil War snowballed into huge and unanticipated dimensions and took on a life and purpose of its own far beyond the causes that had started it. As Lincoln said in his second inaugural address, neither side "expected for the war the magnitude or the duration which it has already attained." Or as he put it on another occasion, "I claim not to have controlled events, but confess plainly that events have controlled me."[27] But in conceding that the war rather than he had shaped the thrust and direction of the revolution, Lincoln was perhaps too modest. For it was his own superb leadership, strategy, and sense of timing as president, commander in chief, and head of the Republican party that determined the pace of the revolution and ensured its success. With a less able man as president, the North might have lost the war or ended it under the leadership of Democrats who would have given its outcome a very different shape. Thus in accepting "the need of dealing with things as they were," Lincoln was not a conservative statesman but a revolutionary statesman.

III Lincoln and Liberty

On April 18, 1864, Abraham Lincoln returned to Baltimore for the first time since he had passed incognito through the city in the middle of the night three years earlier to escape a suspected assassination plot. This time he came in broad daylight, in the full panoply of the presidency, to address the opening ceremonies of the Maryland Sanitary Fair, a fund-raising event for that remarkable Civil War counterpart of the modern Red Cross and USO, the United States Sanitary Commission. Lincoln's visit occurred against a backdrop of three years of grueling, destructive war. It came on the eve of Union military offensives in Virginia and Georgia that were destined to be more lethal and relentless than anything that had gone before. More than a year earlier Lincoln had issued the Emancipation Proclamation, and just ten days before this Baltimore speech the Senate had passed a Thirteenth Amendment to the Constitution, which when enacted by the House and ratified the following year would end chattel slavery forever in the United States.

"The world has never had a good definition of the word liberty, and the American people, just now, are much in want of one," said Lincoln on this occasion. "We all declare for liberty; but in using the same *word* we do not all mean the same *thing*. With some the word liberty may mean for each man to do as he pleases with himself, and the product of his labor; while with others the same may mean for some men to do as they please with other men, and the product of other men's labor. Here are two, not only different, but incompatible things, called by the same name—liberty." Lincoln went on to illustrate his point with a parable about animals. "The shepherd drives the wolf from the sheep's throat," he said, "for which the sheep thanks the shepherd as a *liberator,* while the wolf denounces him for the same act as the destroyer of liberty, especially as the sheep is a black one. Plainly the sheep and the wolf are not agreed upon a definition of the word liberty; and precisely the same difference prevails to-day among us human creatures, even in the North, and all professing to love liberty. Hence we behold the processes by which thousands are daily passing from under the yoke of bondage, hailed by some as the advance of liberty, and bewailed by others as the destruction of all liberty."[1]

The shepherd in this fable was, of course, Lincoln himself; the black sheep was the slave, and the wolf his owner. Lincoln chose to tell this story in a city where three years earlier a regiment of Massachusetts soldiers on their way to defend the capital had been attacked by a mob. This incident produced, among other things, one of the Confederacy's favorite poems, set to music as "Maryland, My Maryland," and written by a native of Baltimore, in which Lincoln is denounced as a "despot" and "tyrant" trying to snuff out liberty in Maryland and the South. Even as Lincoln spoke, in April 1864, Marylanders were debating a proposal to amend their own constitution to abolish slavery in the state— a proposal that split the white population down the middle, with one side supporting it as a step toward liberty, the other condemning it as a despotic blow against liberty. And it was almost exactly a year later that another native of Maryland shot Lincoln in the name of liberty, shouting as he jumped to the stage of Ford's Theater, "Sic semper tyrannis!"—Thus always to tyrants!

To us, today, it seems self-evident that the emancipation of four million slaves from bondage was a great triumph of liberty. But for a majority of white Americans in the Civil War era—until almost the end of the war—this accomplishment represented the antithesis of liberty. This majority of white Americans included most southerners and more than two-fifths of the northerners—the Democrats, who opposed emancipation to the bitter end. It was the outcome of the war that transformed and expanded the concept of liberty to include abolition of slavery, and it was Lincoln who was the principal agent of this transformation.

Lincoln's complaint that the world had never had a good definition of liberty was well founded. The problem is that there are too many definitions. The *Oxford English Dictionary* has eight major definitions of liberty, with historical illustrations. One historian of ideas has recorded some two hundred definitions that run the gamut from natural liberty, civil liberties, intellectual freedom, religious liberty, to toleration of eccentricities or of deviant personal behavior, freedom of the will, and equality of voting rights in republican self-government. The foremost philosopher of liberty in Lincoln's time—perhaps of all time—was John Stuart Mill, who defined liberty as "protection against the tyranny of the political rulers," a concept that involved the limitation "of the power which can be legitimately exercised by the society over the individual." The leading American political scientist of Lincoln's generation, Francis Lieber, defined liberty as "a high degree of untrammeled political action in the citizen, and an acknowledgment of his dignity and his important rights by the government." A modern historian has pointed out that from the beginning Americans have "associated liberty primarily with their rejection of coercive authority," especially the authority of government.[2] The classic statement of American liberty—the Magna Charta of the United States, as it were—is the Declaration of Independence. "All men are created equal," wrote Thomas Jefferson, and "endowed by their Creator with certain unalienable rights," including "life, liberty, and the pursuit of happiness." Governments are instituted "to secure these rights," but they derive "their just powers from the consent of the governed," so that "whenever any form of government becomes destructive of these ends, it is the right of the people to alter or abolish it."

Common to all these definitions of liberty is the assumption that the main sphere of liberty is political, and that the greatest potential threat to the liberties and rights of the individual comes from government itself. Though government is necessary to protect a citizen's liberty, it must also be prevented from becoming so strong or corrupt as to undermine that same liberty. Most American writings about the concept of liberty over the past three centuries have focused on *civil* liberties and their relationship to government. This is scarcely surprising, for the national consciousness—indeed the nation itself—was forged in the struggle for these civil liberties against what Americans considered overweening government power. This consciousness—this struggle—also helps to explain the paradox of the coexistence of American liberty and American slavery.

Many of the founding fathers were preoccupied with the threat of government to liberty. They tended to see all political history, back at least as far as classical Greece and Rome, as a conflict between liberty and power, with liberty usually losing in the end to the aggrandizement of centralized power by a Caesar, a tyrant, an emperor, a king. Republics based on the liberties and equal rights of citizens under law had been fragile and usually short-lived experiments. Eternal vigilance against the aggressions of government was indeed the price of liberty. At great cost, Englishmen from the days of the Magna Charta down to the Glorious Revolution of 1688 had carved out an enlarged sphere of liberty and self-government through their representatives in Parliament, curtailing the powers of the crown in the process. It was these rights and liberties of Englishmen that Americans fought for in their revolution of 1776. It was this fragile experiment in republicanism that they sought to protect against the threat of excessive power, by adopting a bill of rights, by instituting a series of checks and balances and a division of powers within the national government, and by creating a federal system that fragmented power among national, state, and local governments.

Thus when Americans of the revolutionary and post-revolutionary generations spoke of liberty, they usually meant the rights of states and localities, the freedom of the press, of speech, of assembly, of religion, the right to security in person and home against unwarranted search and seizure, the right to bear arms, the right to a trial by jury, the sanctity of property, and the writ of habeas corpus. These were the birthrights, in principle and in practice, of Americans of European descent. A good many of the founding fathers might have considered them the birthrights, in principle at least, of all other Americans as well. They believed that in theory the phrase "All men are created equal" meant just what it said. In a word, they believed the enslavement of Americans of African descent to be wrong, contrary to the ideals of liberty they had fought for in the Revolution.

But they were faced with a condition, not a theory; a reality, not an ideal. The reality was the existence of slavery in all of the colonies that rebelled against Britain and most of the states that ratified the Constitution, a reality rooted a century or more deep in custom, law, and economics. Wherever the economic roots were shallow and the number of slaves was not large—north of the Mason-Dixon line—the libertarian ideology of the Revolution managed to accomplish the abolition of slavery. But south of the line, liberty and slavery grew up together with a diminishing sense of their incompatibility after 1800. By the generation before the Civil War most white southerners—and a good many northerners as well—not only considered liberty and slavery quite compatible, but even believed that the slavery of blacks was essential to the liberty of whites.

One obstacle to applying the concept of liberty to slaves lay in their legal status as property. The right of property was an essential part of the American notion of liberty; as the political scientist Francis Lieber put it, "one of the staunchest principles of civil liberty is the firmest possible protection of individual property." John Adams insisted that "property is surely a right of mankind as really as liberty." Even his radical cousin Sam Adams asked: "What liberty can there be, when property is taken away without consent?"[3] The Fifth Amendment to the Constitution states that no person shall be deprived of "life, liberty, or property, without due process of law." Antislavery people insisted that this provision mandated the *liberty* of black people in the territories, where the national government had jurisdiction; but the Supreme Court, in the Dred Scott decision of 1857, endorsed instead the proslavery position that this Amendment protected the slaveowner's right to take his human *property* into the territories and have it protected there. Slaves, said the Court, were not persons under the Constitution and therefore had no right to liberty. Indeed, in Chief Justice Roger Taney's words, black persons whether slave *or* free "had no rights which the white man was bound to respect."[4]

In another sense also the notion of property inhibited any application of the concept of liberty to slaves. An essential component of liberty under a republican government, as Thomas Jefferson and his followers viewed it, was *independence*. The opposite of independence, of course, was dependence. A man who depended on another for his living was not truly free—he was subject to the authority, to the orders and manipulation, of the man who paid his wages and who therefore dictated the terms of his existence. Independence—and therefore liberty—could be achieved only by the ownership of productive property: a farm, a business, or a trade in which the skilled artisan owned his tools and was paid directly by the purchaser for the fruits of his labor rather than paid wages for his work. Only a society of property-owning farmers, artisans, tradesmen, and professionals could sustain a republican government. The growth of a large class without property would eventually bring down republican self-government and erect a despotism in its place. That is why Jefferson feared the growth of a wage-earning propertyless class as "sores on the body politic." That is why most state constitutions initially required the ownership of property, or at least the paying of taxes, as a qualification for voting. Women were dependent; children were dependent; slaves were dependent; propertyless laborers were dependent. Therefore they were subject to the authority of their husbands, fathers, masters, or employers; that is why they were defined *out* of the body politic of freemen who owned property and enjoyed the civil and political liberty of self-government in a republic.

But with the rise of industrialization and immigration after 1820, a substantial wage-earning class of white men grew up owning little if any property. Various kinds of protests against and responses to this development fueled the politics and political economy of the Jacksonian era. One response was to broaden the definition of political liberty and self-government by eliminating property and tax-paying qualifications for voting in most states. One's labor power became, in effect, a form of property qualifying one for liberty—if you were free, white, twenty-one, and male.

But the notion of independence as a fundamental part of

liberty persisted, and became bound up with racism, especially in the South, to create an ideology of black slavery as the necessary basis of white liberty. The first part of this ideology was the mud-sill philosophy expressed by many southern thinkers in the 1850s, most bluntly by Senator James Hammond of South Carolina in his famous King Cotton speech of 1858. "In all social systems there must be a class to do the menial duties, to perform the drudgery of life," said Hammond. "It constitutes the very mud-sill of society." Turning to senators from northern states, Hammond said that "your whole hireling class of manual laborers and 'operatives,' as you call them, are essentially slaves. The difference between us is, that our slaves are hired for life . . . yours are hired by the day."[5]

Hammond here reformulated the old Jeffersonian theme that liberty required independence—that is, ownership of property. Because most of the unskilled, propertyless workers in the South were black slaves, a larger proportion of southern whites than of northern whites owned real property. But more important, they all owned the most vital property of all, a white skin. This "Herrenvolk democracy"—the equality of all who belonged to the master race—became the perceived basis for white liberty in the South. It was a reading of the Declaration of Independence that said "all *white* men are created equal." As John C. Calhoun, the leading southern political leader, phrased it: "With us the two great divisions of society are not the rich and the poor, but white and black; and all the former, the poor as well as the rich, belong to the upper class, and are respected and treated as equals." Alabama's fire-eating orator William Lowndes Yancey declared in 1860 that "your fathers and my fathers built this government on two ideas. The first is that the white race is the citizen, and the master race, and the white man is the equal of every other white man. The second idea is that the negro is the inferior race."[6] There-

fore, echoed another Alabama political leader, "slavery se-
cures the equality of the white race, and upon its permanent
establishment rests the hope of democratic liberty." Or as
one of the South's leading newspapers, the *Richmond En-
quirer,* put it succinctly in 1856: "Freedom is not possible
without slavery."[7]

This idea was by no means confined to the South alone.
Many northern workingmen shared it—especially Irish immigrants and other wage-earners at the bottom of the social
scale, where they feared competition with blacks, particularly if the slaves were freed and came north looking for
jobs. This fear sparked many of the anti-Negro riots in northern cities from the 1830s to 1860s, including the largest of
all, the New York draft riots of 1863. This Herrenvolk theme
of white supremacy was also a fundamental premise of the
Democratic party. Stephen A. Douglas was one of its principal spokesmen, most notably in his famous debates with
Lincoln in 1858.

For Lincoln rejected the notion that the rights of liberty
and the pursuit of happiness were confined to the white
race. He was not the only American to challenge this dogma,
of course. From the beginning of their movement, abolitionists had insisted that black people were equal to whites in
the sight of God and equally entitled to liberty in this world.
Indeed, the abolitionists and the radical wing of the Republican party went further than Lincoln in maintaining the
principle of equal rights for all people. But because of his
prominence as a Republican party leader after 1858 and his
power as president of the United States after 1860, Lincoln's
were the opinions that mattered most and that are of most
interest to us.

Lincoln had always considered slavery an institution
"founded on both injustice and bad policy," as he told the
Illinois legislature in 1837. But he nevertheless indulged in
the American habit of describing the United States as a "free

country" that enjoyed more "civil and religious liberty," more "human liberty, human right" than any other people in the history of the world. Even as late as 1861 Lincoln could refer to "the free institutions which we have unceasingly enjoyed for three-quarters of a century."[8] But a decade earlier Lincoln had begun to question just how free those institutions were, so long as slavery existed in this otherwise free country. The "monstrous injustice of slavery," he said in 1854, "deprives our republican example of its just influence in the world—enables the enemies of free institutions, with plausibility, to taunt us as hypocrites." In the 1850s Lincoln began to insist, contrary to the belief of perhaps two-thirds of white Americans, that the Declaration of Independence was not merely "the white-man's charter of freedom." "The negro is included in the word 'men' used in the Declaration," he maintained. This "is the great fundamental principle upon which our free institutions rest," and "negro slavery is violative of that principle" because the black man is "entitled to . . . the right to life, liberty, and the pursuit of happiness. I hold that he is as much entitled to these as the white man. I agree with Judge Douglas he is not my equal in many respects"—here Lincoln stopped short of the abolitionist affirmation of full equality—but, Lincoln continued, "in the right to eat the bread, without leave of anybody else, which his own hand earns, he is my equal and the equal of Judge Douglas, and the equal of every living man."[9]

Lincoln did not consider this a new definition of liberty. He believed that Thomas Jefferson and the other founders had meant to include the Negro in the phrase "all men are created equal," even though many of the founders owned slaves, for they were stating a principle that they hoped would eventually become a reality. Douglas maintained that, on the contrary, Jefferson had not meant "all men" to include blacks—nor for that matter any race except Caucasians.

"This government was made by white men, for the benefit of white men and their posterity forever, and should never be administered by any except white men," insisted Douglas over and over again. "The signers of the Declaration had no reference to the negro whatever when they declared all men to be created equal. They . . . [meant] white men, men of European birth and European descent and had no reference either to the negro, the savage Indians, the Fejee, the Malay, or any other inferior and degraded race."[10]

If a national referendum could have been held on these two definitions of liberty—Lincoln's inclusive one and Douglas's definition exclusive of all but white men—Douglas's position would have won. But Lincoln persisted against the odds, denouncing Douglas's argument as representing a disastrous declension from the faith of the fathers, a declension that if it went much further would extinguish the light of liberty in America. The Know-Nothings, for example, were trying to deny to white immigrants the liberties of free-born Americans. Here was the danger, warned Lincoln in 1855. Once a nation decided that its constitutional rights applied only to some and not to all men equally, the torch of liberty would go out. "Our progress in degeneracy appears to me to be pretty rapid," lamented Lincoln with reference to the Know-Nothings. "As a nation, we began by declaring that 'all men are created equal.' We now practically read it 'all men are created equal, except negroes.' When the Know-Nothings get control, it will read 'all men are created equal, except negroes, and foreigners, and catholics.' When it comes to this I should prefer emigrating to some other country where they make no pretence of loving liberty—to Russia, for instance, where despotism can be taken pure, without the base alloy of hypocrisy."[11]

To dehumanize the Negro—to insist that he was not a man—would boomerang on all of us, said Lincoln on many occasions in the 1850s. "Our reliance [must be] in the *love of liberty* . . . the preservation of the spirit which prizes liberty as the heritage of all men, in all lands, every where. Destroy this spirit, and you have planted the seeds of despotism around your own doors. Familiarize yourselves with the chains of bondage, and you are preparing your own limbs to wear them. . . . He who would *be* no slave, must consent to *have* no slave. Those who deny freedom to others, deserve it not for themselves. . . . Accustomed to trample on the rights of those around you, you have lost the genius of your own independence, and become the fit subjects of the first cunning tyrant who rises." The Democratic party of 1859, said Lincoln in that year, had departed so far from the ideas of its founder Thomas Jefferson that it "hold[s] the *liberty* of one man to be absolutely nothing, when in conflict with another man's right of *property*." The only liberty that many whites seemed to believe in was "the liberty of making slaves of other people."[12]

"That is the real issue," said Lincoln in the peroration of his last debate with Douglas. "That is the issue that will continue in this country when these poor tongues of Judge Douglas and myself shall be silent. It is the eternal struggle between these two principles—right and wrong . . . from the beginning of time. . . . The one is the common right of humanity and the other the divine right of kings. . . . No matter in what shape it comes, whether from a king who seeks to bestride the people of his own nation and live by the fruit of their labor, or from one race of men as an apology for enslaving another race, it is the same tyrannical principle." To prevent this principle from "eradicating the light of liberty in this American people," Lincoln pleaded, "let us re-adopt the Declaration of Independence, and with it, the practices, and policy, which harmonize with it. . . . If we do this, we shall not only have saved the Union; but we shall have so saved it, as to make, and to keep it, forever worthy of the saving."[13]

It was Lincoln's eloquent definition—or redefinition—of liberty that the South most feared. So when he won the presidency, southern states seceded in the name of their own liberties of property and state sovereignty, in the name of their right proclaimed by the Declaration of Independence to "alter or abolish" the form of government if it became destructive of the purpose of protecting their property. Southerners, said an Alabama newspaper in 1861, were a "liberty loving people," and therefore "the same spirit of freedom and independence that impelled our Fathers to the separation from the British Government" would inspire the South's fight for independence from a tyrannical and oppressive government dominated by Black Republican Yankees. A Georgia secessionist declared that southerners would be "either *slaves in the Union or freemen out of it.*"[14] One of four brothers from Texas who enlisted in the Confederate army said that like their forefathers of 1776, he and his brothers "are now enlisted in 'The Holy Cause of Liberty and Independence.'" Another Texan called for all true sons of the Lone Star State to rally "to the standard of Liberty and Equality for white men" against "our Abolition enemies who are pledged to prostrate the white freemen of the South down to equality with negroes."[15] And Jefferson Davis appealed to his people to "renew such sacrifices as our fathers bequeathed to us" from "the tyranny of an unbridled majority, the most odious . . . form of despotism."[16]

Antislavery northerners scoffed at southern claims to be acting in the spirit of the Revolution of 1776 for liberty. Secession, they said, was "the oddest Revolution that History has yet seen, a Revolution for the greater security of Injustice, and the firmer establishment of Tyranny!"[17] Lincoln agreed. Even before he committed himself in the second year of the Civil War to emancipation as a war aim, Lincoln repeatedly insisted that it was the North, not the South, that fought to preserve the American heritage of liberty. The republic that the founding fathers had established as a bulwark of liberty was a vulnerable experiment in a world bestrode by kings, emperors, czars, and dictators. Most republics through history had succumbed to counterrevolutions or *coups d'état*. The French republics created by that country's revolutions had twice given way to emperors and had once seen the Bourbon monarchy restored. Republics in Latin America rarely lasted more than a few years. The United States represented, in Lincoln's words, "the last, best hope" for the survival of republican liberties in the world. European conservatives regularly predicted that this upstart democracy would collapse; a successful rebellion by the South would confirm that prediction. "The central idea pervading this struggle," said Lincoln in 1862, "is the necessity that is upon us, of proving that popular government is not an absurdity." The struggle, moreover, was "not altogether for today. It is for a vast future," for it "presents to the whole family of man, the question whether a constitutional republic, a democracy," a nation "conceived in Liberty, and dedicated to the proposition that all men are created equal," as Lincoln expressed it in the Gettysburg Address, "can long endure."[18]

Slavery was not the only problem that involved the question of liberty during the Civil War. In any war the civil liberties of citizens are liable to become victims of the passions or necessities of the conflict. During World War I hundreds of German-Americans, pacifists, and radicals went to jail and tens of thousands of others lost their freedom of speech, press, assembly, and other civil liberties. In the first months of American participation in World War II, the government rounded up and interned more than one hundred thousand Americans whose only crime was their Japanese ancestry. These violations of civil liberties occurred in wars fought far from American shores. The Civil War posed an even greater potential threat to civil liberties. By its very nature a civil war produces a more intense concern with internal security than a foreign war. Martial law prevails over large parts of a country wracked by civil war; newspapers and other media of communication are often muzzled; enemy partisans and sympathizers are arbitrarily arrested and jailed, sometimes tortured and murdered.

Both sides in the American Civil War experienced an erosion of civil liberties during the conflict. One of Lincoln's first wartime orders as commander in chief was to suspend the privilege of the writ of habeas corpus in portions of Maryland wracked by guerrilla activities and mob attacks on Union forces. If the Confederates gained control of Maryland by such actions, the national capital would be surrounded by enemy territory and the North would lose the war before it had fairly started. Union soldiers arrested numerous pro-southern citizens in Maryland, including the mayor and police chief of Baltimore and thirty-one members of the state legislature, and clapped them in prison for months and in a few cases for more than a year without trial. Lincoln eventually extended the suspension of the writ of habeas corpus to the whole country in cases of what he defined as "disloyal persons [who] are not adequately restrained by the ordinary processes of law from . . . giving aid and comfort in various ways to the insurrection."[19] By the time the war was over, Union soldiers had arrested and detained in prison without charge at least fifteen thousand civilians, while military courts had tried and convicted hundreds of others.

Most of these arrests took place in the border slave states of Maryland, Kentucky, and Missouri, where loyalties were divided and active fighting was going on, or in portions of Confederate states occupied by conquering Union forces. Most of those arrested had in fact engaged in activities with military significance, such as guerrilla attacks on Union soldiers, burning of bridges, blowing up of supply dumps, espionage, and the like. But some men were arrested for merely speaking or writing in favor of peace with the Confederacy or against the war policies of the Union government. Some of those arrested lived in northern states far from active war zones. One of the most notorious wartime violations of civil liberties occurred in Ohio where a military court convicted Democratic gubernatorial candidate Clement L. Vallandigham of treason for speaking out against the war. Lincoln commuted the sentence from imprisonment to banishment, and Vallandigham went to Canada, from where he conducted his unsuccessful campaign for governor of Ohio. Another celebrated case concerned one Lambdin P. Milligan, an Indiana civilian who was convicted of treason by a military court in 1864 for aiding Confederate agents trying to foment an uprising in the North. After the war the Supreme Court overturned Milligan's conviction in a ruling that civilians cannot be tried by military courts in a region where the regularly established courts of the land are functioning, as they were in Indiana. Constitutional historians regard the *Milligan* decision as a landmark in the defense of civil liberties; some of them also interpret it as a rebuke to the Lincoln administration's record on this issue.

There was no shortage of such rebukes during the Civil War itself. In fact, northern Democrats made this issue the central theme in their attacks on Lincoln as a despot, a tyrant bent on snuffing out the liberties of white men in a calamitous and unconstitutional crusade to liberate black slaves. Countless Democratic speeches and editorials, especially at the time of Vallandigham's arrest, condemned Lincoln for suppressing "the right of the people to assemble and discuss the affairs of government, the liberty of speech and of the press, the right of trial by jury," for violating "the rights of the States and the liberties of the citizen," and for "establishing a despotism." Was the government, asked a group of New York Democrats in 1863, trying to suppress rebellion in the South or "to destroy free institutions in the North"?[20] A Democratic pamphlet published in 1863 portrayed Lincoln as standing trial before the founding fathers. They find him guilty. "You were born in the freest country under the sun," they tell the sixteenth president, "but you have converted it into a despotism. [We] now leave you, with the brand of TYRANT upon your brow."[21]

Is this how we, too, should leave Lincoln? Perhaps we should first let him speak in his own defense. Hear him on the suspension of the writ of habeas corpus, for example. By protecting individuals from arbitrary arrest and imprisonment without indictment and trial, this writ has been the safeguard of Anglo-American civil liberties for centuries. The United States Constitution specifies that the privilege of the writ of habeas corpus "shall not be suspended, except when in cases of rebellion or invasion the public safety may require it." But this rebellion, said Lincoln in 1861, was precisely the kind of exceptional crisis the framers had in mind. Chief Justice Taney—author of the Dred Scott decision—insisted that only Congress, and not the president acting in executive capacity, had the power to suspend the writ. Lincoln disagreed, and many constitutional scholars then and since have supported his position. Suspension of the writ was an emergency power; only the executive could act quickly enough in a crisis, especially if Congress was not in session. The very life of the nation was at stake, Lincoln maintained. The survival of that nation "conceived in liberty and dedicated to the proposition that all men are created equal," was the central purpose of the war. If the nation died, so did the fragile experiment in republican liberty launched in 1776. Thus the temporary suspension of habeas corpus, said Lincoln in his first message to Congress on July 4, 1861, was a small price to pay for the preservation of that larger framework of liberty, the nation itself. "Are all the laws but one [habeas corpus] to go unexecuted," asked Lincoln rhetorically, "and the government itself go to pieces, lest that one be violated?" Using a metaphor as he often did with great effect, Lincoln sought to allay fears that the emergency suspension of certain civil liberties during wartime would create precedents fatal to liberty in peacetime: he could no more believe that this would happen, he said, than he could "believe that a man could contract so strong an appetite for emetics during temporary illness, as to persist in feeding upon them through the remainder of his healthful life."[22]

In any event, said Lincoln, most of the military arrests of civilians were for military crimes such as sabotage, espionage, and guerrilla bushwhacking. "Under cover of 'liberty of speech,' 'liberty of the press,' and 'Habeas corpus,'" he continued, the rebels "hoped to keep on foot amongst us a most efficient corps of spies, informers, suppliers, and aiders and abettors of their cause." As for the few conspicuous cases of arrests of politicians like Vallandigham or of newspaper editors for speaking out against the war or the draft, Lincoln argued that their speeches and editorials discouraged enlistment in the army or encouraged desertions from it, thereby "damaging the army, upon the existence and vigor of which the life of the nation depends." In a rhetorical question that became one of the most famous of Lincoln's utterances, he asked: "Must I shoot a simple-minded soldier boy who deserts, while I must not touch a hair of a wily agitator who induces him to desert? . . . I think that in such a case to silence the agitator and save the boy is not only constitutional, but withal a great mercy."[23]

Such arguments did little to assuage Lincoln's critics or persuade his opponents. They saw his record on civil liberties as only part of a larger pattern of threats to traditional American liberties. Two other parts of the pattern were conscription and emancipation. Conscription, they said, robbed the citizen of a choice whether or not to serve in the army;

emancipation took away the citizen's property without due process of law.

How do we, as students of history, respond to this indictment? Where do we come down on the question of Lincoln and Liberty? Do we agree with Lincoln himself that preservation of the republic created in 1776 was essential to the survival of liberty, and that all else was a necessary means to this end even if the means included a temporary suspension of some civil liberties? Do we point out that no society in the last three hundred years has been able to fight a major war without some kind of conscription, that the draft in the Civil War raised directly only 10 to 15 percent of the soldiers in the Union army, the rest of whom were volunteers, and that with its many loopholes the draft fell more lightly on the northern people than on any other people at war in modern times? Do we also point out that compared with the harassment and imprisonment of dissidents during World War I or the internment of Japanese-Americans in World War II, the Lincoln administration's violation of civil liberties during the much greater crisis of the Civil War seems quite mild indeed? As for emancipation, are we today more likely to identify with those four million black sheep liberated by Lincoln or with the loss of liberty by four hundred thousand wolves to prey on those sheep?

But there is a larger question involved here—nothing less than a transformation in the concept of liberty itself. To illustrate this point, let us turn to the definitions offered by the British philosopher Isaiah Berlin in a famous essay, "Two Concepts of Liberty."[24] The two concepts are Negative Liberty and Positive Liberty. The idea of negative liberty is perhaps more familiar. It can be defined as the absence of restraint, a freedom from interference by outside authority with individual thought or behavior. A law requiring motorcyclists to wear a helmet would be, under this definition, to prevent them from enjoying the freedom to go bare-headed if they wish. Negative liberty, therefore, can be described as freedom *from*. Positive liberty can best be understood as freedom *to*. It is not necessarily incompatible with negative liberty, but has a different focus or emphasis. Freedom of the press is generally viewed as a negative liberty—freedom from interference with what a writer writes or a reader reads. But an illiterate person suffers from a denial of positive liberty; he is unable to enjoy the freedom to write or read whatever he pleases, not because some authority prevents him from doing so, but because he cannot read or write anything. He suffers not the absence of a negative liberty—freedom from—but of a positive liberty—freedom *to* read and write. The remedy lies not in removal of restraint but in achievement of the capacity to read and write.

Another way of defining the distinction between these two concepts of liberty is to describe their relation to power.[25] Negative liberty and power are at opposite poles; power is the enemy of liberty, especially power concentrated in the hands of a central government. That is the kind of power that many of the founding fathers feared most; that is why they fragmented power in the Constitution and the federal system; that is why they wrote a bill of rights to restrain the power of the national government to interfere with individual liberty. The Bill of Rights is an excellent example of negative liberty. Nearly all of the first ten amendments to the Constitution apply the phrase "shall not" to the federal government. In fact, eleven of the first twelve amendments placed limitations on the power of the national government. But beginning with the Thirteenth Amendment in 1865—the Amendment that abolished slavery—six of the next seven amendments radically expanded the power of the federal government at the expense of the states. The very language of these amendments illustrates the point: instead of applying the phrase "shall not" to the national government, every one of them grants significant new powers to the government with the phrase that "Congress *shall have* the power to enforce this article" (italics added).

These six amendments did not all necessarily enlarge the sphere of liberty. The Sixteenth authorized a federal income tax and the Eighteenth prohibited the manufacture and sale of alcoholic beverages. Some of their supporters regarded these amendments as expanding the sphere of positive liberty, by increasing the potential of the federal government to redistribute income and provide social welfare, thereby improving the condition of the poor, and by ending the "enslavement" of millions of Americans to liquor. Whatever the validity of these arguments, the other four constitutional amendments do offer examples of positive liberty. They nicely illustrate the relationship between positive liberty and power. Power in these cases expanded liberty instead of repressing it; power and liberty were allies, not enemies. The emphasis was not on freedom from, but freedom to. These four amendments represent a positive expansion of liberty in another respect as well. They define *into* the population enjoying certain rights and liberties large groups that had been previously defined *out:* black people and women. The Thirteenth, Fourteenth, and Fifteenth Amendments freed the slaves and granted blacks equal civil and political rights; the Nineteenth granted women equal political rights.

Abraham Lincoln played a crucial role in this historic shift of emphasis from negative to positive liberty. Those southerners who seceded from the Union in the name of preserving their liberties and rights—including the right to own slaves—and those northerners who denounced the Lincoln administration for violating their civil liberties, were acting in the tradition of negative liberty. Let us return to Lincoln's parable of the shepherd, the wolf, and the sheep quoted at the beginning of this essay. "The shepherd drives the wolf from the sheep's throat, for which the sheep thanks the shepherd as a liberator." Here is Lincoln the shepherd using the great power of government and the army to achieve a positive liberty for the sheep. But the wolf was a believer in negative liberty, for to him the shepherd was "the destroyer of liberty, especially as the sheep was a black one."

Positive liberty is an open-ended concept. It has the capacity to expand toward notions of equity, justice, social welfare, equality of opportunity. For how much liberty does a starving person enjoy, except the liberty to starve? How much freedom of the press can exist in a society of illiterate people? How free is a motorcyclist who is paralyzed for life by a head injury that might have been prevented if he had worn a helmet? With the "new birth of freedom" proclaimed in the Gettysburg Address and backed by a powerful army, Lincoln helped to move the nation toward an expanded and open-ended concept of positive liberty. "On the side of the Union," he said on another occasion, this war "is a struggle for maintaining in the world, that form, and substance of government, whose leading object is, to elevate the condition of men—to lift artificial weights from all shoulders—to clear the paths of laudable pursuit for all"—black as well as white—"to afford all, an unfettered start, and a fair chance, in the race of life." In "giving freedom to the slave," declared Lincoln, "we *assure* freedom to the *free*."[26]

IV   Lincoln and the Strategy of Unconditional Surrender

It is ironic that one of the most oft-quoted passages from Lincoln's writings is the concluding paragraph of his second inaugural address. "With malice toward none," said Lincoln, "with charity for all," let us "bind up the nation's wounds" and strive to "achieve and cherish a just, and a lasting peace."[1] These words have helped shape Lincoln's image as a man of compassion and mercy who desired a magnanimous peace. This image is true enough; but it is only part of the truth. While Lincoln did want a soft peace, he had recognized long before 1865 that it could be achieved only by a hard war. And he insisted on the unconditional surrender of Confederate forces before he would even talk of peace.

The fact is, the overwhelming circumstance shaping Lincoln's presidency was war. He had been willing to risk war rather than let the nation perish. *He was a war president.* Indeed, he was the only president in our history whose entire administration was bounded by the parameters of war. The first official document that Lincoln saw as president—on the morning after the inaugural ball—was a letter from Major Robert Anderson at Fort Sumter stating that unless resupplied he could hold out only a few more weeks. This news, in effect, struck the first blow of the Civil War;

the fatal shot fired by John Wilkes Booth on April 14, 1865, struck virtually the last blow of the war. During the intervening one thousand, five hundred and three days there was scarcely one in which Lincoln was not preoccupied with the war. Military matters took up more of his time and attention than any other matter, as indicated by the activities chronicled in that fascinating volume, *Lincoln Day by Day*.[2] He spent more time in the War Department telegraph office than anywhere else except the White House itself. During times of crisis, Lincoln frequently stayed at the telegraph office all night reading dispatches from the front, sending dispatches of his own, holding emergency conferences with Secretary of War Stanton, General-in-Chief Halleck, and other officials. He wrote the first draft of the Emancipation Proclamation in this office while awaiting news from the army.[3] This was appropriate, for the legal justification of the proclamation was its "military necessity" as a war measure.

Lincoln took seriously his constitutional duty as commander in chief of the army and navy. He borrowed books on military strategy from the Library of Congress and burned the midnight oil reading them. No fewer than eleven times he left Washington to visit the Army of the Potomac at the fighting front in Virginia or Maryland, spending a total of forty-two days with that army. Some of the most dramatic events in Lincoln's presidency grew out of his direct intervention in strategic and command decisions. In May 1862, along with Secretary of War Stanton and Secretary of the Treasury Chase, he visited Union forces at Hampton Roads in Virginia and personally issued orders that led to the occupation of Norfolk. Later that same month, Lincoln haunted the War Department telegraph room almost around the clock for more than a week and fired off a total of fifty telegrams to half a dozen generals to coordinate an attempt to trap and crush Stonewall Jackson's army in the Shenandoah Valley—an attempt that failed partly because Jackson moved too fast but mainly because Union generals, much to Lincoln's disgust, moved too slowly. A couple of months later, Lincoln made the controversial decision to transfer the Army of the Potomac from the Virginia peninsula southeast of Richmond to northern Virginia covering Washington. And a couple of months later yet, Lincoln finally removed General George B. McClellan from command of this army because McClellan seemed reluctant to fight. A year later, in September 1863, Lincoln was roused from bed at his summer residence in a Maryland suburb of Washington for a dramatic midnight conference at the War Department where he decided to send four divisions from the Army of the Potomac to reinforce General William S. Rosecrans's besieged army in Chattanooga after it had lost the battle of Chickamauga.

Lincoln subsequently put Ulysses S. Grant in command at Chattanooga and then in the spring of 1864 brought him to Washington as the new general in chief. Thereafter, with a commander in charge who had Lincoln's full confidence, the president played a less direct role in command decisions than he had done before. Nevertheless, Lincoln continued to help shape crucial strategic plans and to sustain Grant against pressures from all sides during that dark summer of 1864. "It is the dogged pertinacity of Grant that wins," the president told his private secretary. Lincoln wired Grant in Virginia during the terrible fighting at Petersburg: "I begin to see it. You will succeed. God bless you all."[4] When Confederate General Jubal Early drove a small Union army out of the Shenandoah Valley in the summer of 1864, crossed the Potomac, and threatened Washington itself before being driven off, Lincoln went personally to Fort Stevens, part of the Washington defenses, to observe the fighting. It was on this occasion that a Union officer standing a few feet from Lincoln was hit by a Confederate bullet and that another officer—none other than Oliver Wendell Holmes, Jr.—

noting without recognizing out of the corner of his eye this tall civilian standing on the parapet in the line of fire, said urgently: "Get down, you damn fool, before you get shot!" A chastened president got down.[5]

Grant subsequently sent several divisions from the Army of the Potomac with orders to go after Early's army in the Shenandoah Valley "and follow him to the death." When Lincoln saw these orders he telegraphed Grant: "This, I think, is exactly right." But "it will neither be done nor attempted unless you watch it every day, and hour, and force it."[6] In response to this telegram Grant came to Washington, conferred with Lincoln, and put his most trusted subordinate, Philip Sheridan, in command of the Union forces in the Shenandoah Valley where they did indeed follow Early to the death of his army. About the same time, Lincoln approved the plans for Sherman's march through Georgia. It was these three campaigns—Grant's chewing and choking of Lee's army at Petersburg, Sheridan's following of Early to the death in the Valley, and Sherman's march through Georgia and the Carolinas—that finally destroyed the Confederacy and brought about its unconditional surrender.

Commander-in-Chief Lincoln was mainly responsible for this unconditional victory of Union forces. But in the huge body of writing about Lincoln—there are said to be more titles in the English language about Lincoln than about anyone else except Jesus and Shakespeare—a relatively small number of books and articles focus primarily on Lincoln as a war leader. In 1982 Mark Neely, Jr., completed *The Abraham Lincoln Encyclopedia,* a valuable compendium of informaton and scholarship—which devotes less than 5 percent of its space to military and related matters. In September 1984, Gettysburg College hosted a conference on recent scholarship about the sixteenth president. This conference had three sessions on books of psychohistory about Lincoln, two sessions on books about his assassination, two sessions on Lincoln's image in photographs and popular prints, one on his economic ideas, one on Lincoln and civil religion, one on his humor, one on his Indian policy, and one on slavery and emancipation—but no session on Lincoln as commander in chief. In 1987 the outstanding Lincoln scholar of our time, Don E. Fehrenbacher, published a collection of essays, *Lincoln in Text and Context*. Of its seventeen essays on Lincoln, none dealt with the president as a military leader.[7] This is not intended as criticism of these enterprises, which are superb achievements in writings about Lincoln. Rather, it is a reflection on the nature and direction of modern Lincoln scholarship.

In the 1950s, fine studies by two historians named Williams—T. Harry and Kenneth P.—told us everything we might want to know about Lincoln's search for the right military strategy and for the right generals to carry it out.[8] A number of other books and articles have also explored Lincoln's relationships with his generals, the wisdom or lack thereof that the president demonstrated in certain strategic decisions, and a great deal more of a similar nature. Many of these are excellent studies. They provide important and fascinating insights on Lincoln as commander in chief. But as a portrait of Lincoln the strategist of Union victory, they are incomplete. The focus is too narrow; the larger picture is somehow blurred.

Most of these studies are based on too restricted a definition of strategy. On this matter we can consult with profit the writings of the most influential theorist of war, Carl von Clausewitz. One of Clausewitz's famous maxims defines war as the continuation of state policy by other means—that is, war is an instrument of last resort to achieve a nation's political goals. Using this insight, we can divide our definition of strategy into two parts: First, *national strategy* (or what the British call grand strategy); second, *military strategy* (or what the British call operational strategy). National strategy is the shaping and defining of a nation's political goals in time of war. Military strategy is the use of armed forces to achieve those goals.[9] Most studies of Lincoln and his generals focus mainly on this second kind of strategy—that is, military or operational strategy. And that is the problem. For it is impossible to understand military strategy without also comprehending national strategy—the political war aims—for which military strategy is merely the instrument. This is true to some degree in all wars; it was especially true of the American Civil War, which was pre-eminently a *political* war precipitated by a presidential election in the world's most politicized society, fought largely by volunteer soldiers who elected many of their officers and who also helped elect the political leadership that directed the war effort, and in which many of the commanders were appointed for political reasons.

Let us look at this matter of political generals, to illustrate the point that military strategy can be understood only within the larger context of national strategy. Both Abraham Lincoln and Jefferson Davis appointed generals who had little or no professional training: men like Benjamin Butler, Nathaniel Banks, Carl Schurz, Robert Toombs, Henry Wise, and so on. A good many of these generals proved to be incompetent; some battlefield disasters resulted from their presence in command. Professional army officers bemoaned the prominence of political generals: Henry W. Halleck, for example, commented that "it seems but little better than murder to give important commands to such men as Banks, Butler, McClernand, and Lew Wallace, but it seems impossible to prevent it."[10]

A good many military historians have similarly deplored the political generals. They often cite one anecdote to ridicule the process. To satisfy the large German ethnic constituency in the North, Lincoln felt it necessary to name a number of German-American generals. Poring over a list of eligible men one day in 1862, the president came across the name of Alexander Schimmelfennig. "The very man!" said Lincoln. When Secretary of War Stanton protested that better-qualified officers were available, the president insisted on Schimmelfennig. "His name," said Lincoln, "will make up for any difference there may be," and he walked away repeating the name Schimmelfennig with a chuckle.[11]

Historians who note that Schimmelfennig turned out to be a mediocre commander miss the point. Their criticism is grounded in a narrow concept of *military* strategy. But Lincoln made this and similar appointments for reasons of *national* strategy. Each of the political generals represented an important ethnic, regional, or political constituency in the North. The support of these constituencies for the war effort was crucial. Democrats, Irish-Americans, many German-Americans, and most residents of the watershed of the Ohio River had not voted for Lincoln in 1860 and were potential defectors from a war to crush the rebels and coerce the South back into the Union. To mobilize their support for this war, Lincoln had to give them political patronage; a general's commission was one of the highest patronage plums. From the viewpoint of military strategy this may have been inefficient; from the viewpoint of national strategy it was essential.

And even in the narrower military sense the political patronage system produced great benefits for the North, for without it Ulysses S. Grant and William T. Sherman might not have gotten their start up the chain of command. Although West Point graduates, both men had resigned from the pre-war army and neither was conspicuous at the outbreak of the war. But Sherman happened to be the brother of an influential Republican senator and Grant happened to be an acquaintance of an influential Republican congressman from Illinois. These fortuitous political connections helped get them their initial commissions in the army. The rest is history—but had it not been for the political dictates of national strategy, they might never have made their mark on the history of military strategy.

Clausewitz describes two kinds of national strategy in war. One is the conquest of a certain amount of the enemy's territory or the defense of one's own territory from conquest. The second is the overthrow of the enemy's political system. The first usually means a limited war ended by a negotiated peace. The second usually means a total war ending in unconditional surrender by the loser.[12] These are absolute or ideal types, of course; in the real world some wars are a mixture of both types. In American history most of our wars have been mainly of the first, limited type: the Revolution, which did seek the overthrow of British political power in the thirteen colonies but not elsewhere; the War of 1812; the Mexican War; the Spanish-American War; the Korean War. American goals in World War I were mixed: primarily they involved the limited aims of defending the territory and right of self-government of European nationalities, but in effect this required the overthrow of the German and Austro-Hungarian monarchies. In Vietnam the American goal was mainly the limited one of defending the territory and sovereignty of South Vietnam and its anti-Communist government, but this was mixed with the purpose of overthrowing the political system that prevailed in part of South Vietnam and involved attacks on that system in North Vietnam as well.

World War II and the Civil War were the two unalloyed examples in American history of Clausewitz's second type of war—total war ending in unconditional surrender and the overthrow of the enemy's political system. These wars were also "total" in the sense that they mobilized the society's whole population and resources for a prolonged conflict that ended only when the armed forces and resources of one side were totally destroyed or exhausted.

Common sense, not to mention Clausewitz, will tell us that there should be congruity between national and military strategy. That is, an all-out war to overthrow the enemy requires total mobilization plus a military strategy to destroy the enemy's armies, resources, and morale, while a limited war requires a limited strategy to gain or defend territory. When natonal and military strategy become inconsistent with each other—when the armed forces adopt or want to adopt an unlimited military strategy to fight a limited war, or vice versa—then a nation fights at cross purposes, with dissension or failure the likely outcome. This can happen when a war that is initially limited in purpose takes on a momentum, a life of its own that carries the participants beyond their original commitment without a proper redefinition of war aims—for example World War I, which became a total war in military strategy without a concomitant redefinition of national strategy and ended with an armistice rather than with unconditional surrender. But it produced a peace treaty that Germany resented as a *Diktat* because it treated the Germans as if they had surrendered unconditionally. This in turn generated a stab-in-the-back legend that facilitated the rise of Hitler.

One of the reasons the Allied powers in World War II insisted on unconditional surrender was their determination that this time there must be no armistice, no stab-in-the-back legend, no doubt on the part of the defeated peoples that they had been utterly beaten and their Fascist governments overthrown. The Allies won World War II because they had a clear national strategy and a military strategy in harmony with it—along with the resources to do the job. In the Korean War, disharmony between President Truman, who insisted on a limited war, and General MacArthur, who wanted to fight an unlimited one, resulted in MacArthur's dismissal and a sense of frustration among many Americans who wanted to overthrow the Communist government of

North Korea and perhaps of China as well. In Vietnam, the controversy and failure resulted from an inability of the government to define clearly the American national strategy. This inability resulted in turn from deep and bitter divisions in American society over the national purpose in this conflict. Without a clear national strategy to guide them, the armed forces could not develop an effective military strategy.

The Civil War confronted the Union government with these same dangers of unclear national strategy and a consequent confusion of purpose between national and military strategy. Like World War I, the Civil War started out as one kind of war and evolved into something quite different. But in contrast to World War I, the government of the victorious side in the Civil War developed a national strategy to give purpose to a military strategy of total war, and preserved a political majority in support of this national strategy through dark days of defeat, despair, and division. This was the real strategic contribution of Abraham Lincoln to Union victory. His role in shaping a national strategy of unconditional surrender by the Confederacy was more important to the war's outcome than his endless hours at the War Department sending telegrams to generals and devising strategic combinations to defeat Confederate armies.

In one sense, from the beginning the North fought Clausewitz's second type of war—to overthrow the enemy's government—for the northern war aim was to bring Confederate states back into the Union. But Lincoln waged this war on the legal theory that since secession was unconstitutional, southern states were still *in* the Union and the Confederate government was not a legitimate government. Lincoln's first war action, the proclamation of April 15, 1861, calling for 75,000 militia to serve for ninety days, declared that their purpose would be to "suppress . . . combinations too powerful to be suppressed by the ordinary course of judicial proceedings."[13] In other words this was a domestic insurrection, a rebellion by certain lawless citizens, not a war between nations. Throughout the war Lincoln maintained this legal fiction; he never referred to Confederate states or to Confederates, but to rebel states and rebels. Thus, the North fought the war not on the theory of overthrowing an enemy state or even conquering enemy territory, but of suppressing insurrection and restoring authority in its own territory. This national strategy was based on an assumption that a majority of the southern people were loyal to the Union and that eleven states had been swept into secession by the passions of the moment. Once the United States demonstrated its firmness by regaining control of its forts and other property in the South, those presumed legions of loyal Unionists would regain political control of their states and resume their normal allegiance to the United States. In his first message to Congress, nearly three months after the firing on Fort Sumter, Lincoln questioned "whether there is, to-day, a majority of the legally qualified voters of any State, except perhaps South Carolina, in favor of disunion." And to show that he would temper firmness with restraint, Lincoln promised that while suppressing insurrection the federalized militia would avoid "any devastation, any destruction of, or interference with, property, or any disturbance of peaceful citizens."[14]

This was a national strategy of limited war—very limited, indeed scarcely war at all, but a police action to quell a rather large riot. This limited national strategy required a limited military strategy. General-in-Chief Winfield Scott—himself a loyal Virginian who shared the government's faith in southern unionism—came up with such a strategy, which was soon labeled the Anaconda Plan. This plan called for a blockade of southern ports by the navy and a campaign down the Mississippi by a combined army and fresh-water naval task force to split the Confederacy and surround most of it with a blue cordon. Having thus sealed off the rebels from the world, Scott would squeeze them firmly—like an Anaconda snake—but with restraint until southerners came to their senses and returned to the Union.

Lincoln approved this plan, which remained a part of northern military strategy through the war. But he also yielded to public pressure to invade Virginia, attack the rebel force at Manassas, and capture Richmond before the Confederate Congress met there in July. This went beyond the Anaconda Plan, but was still part of a limited-war strategy to regain United States territory and disperse the illegitimate rebel Congress in order to put down the rebellion within ninety days. But this effort led to the humiliating Union defeat at Bull Run and to an agonizing reappraisal by the North of the war's scope and strategy. It was now clear that this might be a long, hard war requiring more fighting and a greater mobilization of resources than envisioned by the restrained squeezing of the Anaconda Plan. Congress authorized the enlistment of a million three-year volunteers; by early 1862 nearly 700,000 northerners as well as more than 300,000 southerners were under arms. This was no longer a police action to suppress rioters, but a full-scale war.

Its legal character had also changed, by actions of the Lincoln administration itself. The blockade, for example, called into question the "domestic insurrection" theory of the conflict, for a blockade was recognized by international law as an instrument of war between sovereign nations. Moreover, after first stating an intention to execute captured crewmen of southern privateers as pirates, the administration backed down when the Confederate government threatened to retaliate by executing Union prisoners of war. Captured privateer crews as well as soldiers became prisoners of war. In 1862 the Union government also agreed to a cartel for the exchange of war prisoners, another proceeding rec-

ognized by international law as a form of agreement between nations at war.

Thus, by 1862 the Lincoln administration had, in effect,
conceded that this conflict was a war between belligerent
governments each in control of a large amount of territory.
Nevertheless, the northern war aim was still restoration of
national authority over territory controlled by rebels but not
the overthrow of their fundamental political or social institutions. This limited-war aim called for a limited military
strategy of conquering and occupying territory—Clausewitz's
first type of war. From the fall of 1861 to the spring of 1862,
Union forces enjoyed a great deal of success in this effort.
With the help of local Unionists they gained control of
western Virginia and detached it from the Confederacy to
form the new Union state of West Virginia. The Union navy
with army support gained footholds along the south Atlantic
coast from Norfolk to St. Augustine. The navy achieved its
most spectacular success with the capture of New Orleans
in April 1862 while army troops occupied part of southern
Louisiana. Meanwhile, two Union naval forces drove up and
down the Mississippi until they gained control of all of it
except a 200-mile stretch between Vicksburg, Mississippi
and Port Hudson, Louisiana. Union armies under Ulysses S.
Grant and Don Carlos Buell, supported by river gunboats,
captured Forts Henry and Donelson, occupied Nashville and
most of Tennessee, penetrated far up the Tennessee River
into northern Alabama, and defeated a Confederate coun-
terattack in the bloody battle of Shiloh. In May 1862, the
large and well-trained Army of the Potomac under George
B. McClellan drove Confederates all the way up the Virginia
Peninsula to within five miles of Richmond while panic
seized the southern capital and the Confederate government
prepared to evacuate it. The war for southern independence
seemed to be tottering to defeat. The *New York Tribune*
proclaimed in May 1862 that "the rebels themselves are

panic-stricken, or despondent. It now requires no very far-reaching prophet to predict the end of this struggle."[15]

But the *Tribune* proved to be a poor prophet. The Confederacy picked itself up from the floor and fought back. Guerrilla attacks and cavalry raids in Tennessee and Mississippi struck Union supply bases and transport networks. Stonewall Jackson drove the Federals out of the Shenandoah Valley. Robert E. Lee drove them away from Richmond and off the Peninsula. In the western theater Vicksburg foiled the initial Union efforts to capture it and open the Mississippi. Confederate generals Braxton Bragg and Kirby Smith maneuvered the Yankees out of Tennessee and invaded Kentucky at the same time that Lee smashed them at second Manassas and invaded Maryland. In four months Confederate armies had counterpunched so hard that they had Union forces on the ropes. The limited-war strategy of conquering southern territory clearly would not do the job so long as Confederate armies remained intact and strong.

General Grant was one of the first to recognize this. Before the battle of Shiloh, easy northern victories at Forts Henry and Donelson and elsewhere in the West had convinced him that the Confederacy was a hollow shell about to collapse. After the rebels had counterattacked and nearly ruined him at Shiloh, however, Grant said that he "gave up all idea of saving the Union except by complete conquest."[16] By complete conquest he meant not merely occupation of territory, but destruction of enemy armies, which thereafter became Grant's chief strategic goal. It became Lincoln's goal too. "Destroy the rebel army," he instructed McClellan before the battle of Antietam. When McClellan proved unable or unwilling to do so, Lincoln removed him from command. In 1863, Lincoln told General Joseph Hooker that "Lee's *army*, and not *Richmond*, is your true objective point." When Lee again invaded the North, Lincoln instructed Hooker that this "gives you back the chance [to

destroy the enemy far from his base] that I thought Mc-
Clellan lost last fall." When Hooker hesitated and complained, Lincoln replaced him with George G. Meade who
won the battle of Gettysburg but failed to pursue and attack Lee vigorously as Lincoln implored him to do. "Great
God!" exclaimed the distraught president when he learned
that Meade had let Lee get back across the Potomac without further damage. "Our Army held the war in the hollow
of their hand and would not close it."[17] Lincoln did not
remove Meade, but brought Grant east to oversee him while
leaving Sherman in command in the West. By 1864, Lincoln
finally had generals in top commands who believed in
destroying enemy armies.

This was a large step toward total war, but it was not the
final step. When Grant said that Shiloh convinced him that
the rebellion could be crushed only by complete conquest,
he added that this included the destruction of any property
or other resources used to sustain Confederate armies as
well as of those armies themselves. Before Shiloh, wrote
Grant in his memoirs, he had been careful "to protect the
property of the citizens whose territory was invaded"; after-
wards his policy was to "consume everything that could
be used to support or supply armies." Grant's principal
subordinate in the western theater was Sherman, whose
experiences in Tennessee and Mississippi, where guerrillas
sheltered by the civilian population wreaked havoc behind
Union lines, convinced him that "we are not only fighting hostile armies, but a hostile people, and must make
[them] . . . feel the hard hand of war."[18]

Confiscation of enemy property used in support of war
was a recognized belligerent right under international law;
by the summer of 1862, Union armies in the South had begun to do this on a large scale. The war had come a long
way since Lincoln's initial promise "to avoid any devastation,
any destruction of, or interference with, property." Now

even civilian property such as crops in the field or livestock in the barn was fair game, since these things could be used to feed Confederate armies. Congress approved this policy with a limited confiscation act in August 1861 and a more sweeping act in July 1862. General-in-Chief Halleck gave shape to the policy in August 1862 with orders to Grant about treatment of Confederate sympathizers in Union-occupied territory. "Handle that class without gloves," Halleck told Grant, and "take their property for public use. . . . It is time that they should begin to feel the presence of the war."[19]

Lincoln also endorsed this bare-knuckle policy by the summer of 1862. He had come around slowly to such a position, for it did not conform to the original national strategy of slapping rebels on the wrist with one hand while gently beckoning the hosts of southern Unionists back into the fold with the other. In his message to Congress on December 3, 1861, Lincoln had deprecated radical action against southern property. "In considering the policy to be adopted for suppressing the insurrection," he said, "I have been anxious and careful that the inevitable conflict for this purpose shall not degenerate into a violent and remorseless revolutionary struggle."[20] But during the epic campaigns and battles of 1862, the war did become violent and remorseless, and it would soon become revolutionary.

Like Grant, Lincoln lost faith in those illusory southern Unionists and became convinced that the rebellion could be put down only by complete conquest. To a southern Unionist and a northern conservative who complained in July 1862 about the government's seizure of civilian property and suppression of civil liberties in occupied Louisiana, Lincoln replied angrily that those supposed Unionists had had their chance to overcome the rebel faction in Louisiana and had done nothing but grumble about the army's vigorous enforcement of Union authority. "The paralysis—the dead palsy—of the government in this whole struggle," said Lincoln, "is that this class of men will do nothing for the government, nothing for themselves, except demand that the government shall not strike its open enemies, lest they be struck by accident!" The administration could no longer pursue "a temporizing and forbearing" policy toward the South, said Lincoln. Conservatives and southerners who did not like the new policy should blame the rebels who started the war. They must understand, said Lincoln sternly, "that they cannot experiment for ten years trying to destroy the government, and if they fail still come back into the Union unhurt."[21]

This exchange concerned slavery as well as other kinds of southern property. Slaves were the South's most valuable and vulnerable form of property. Lincoln's policy toward slavery became a touchstone of the evolution of this conflict from a limited war to restore the old Union to a total war to destroy the southern social as well as political system.

During 1861, Lincoln reiterated his oft-repeated pledge that he had no intention of interfering with slavery in the states where it already existed. In July of that year Congress endorsed this position by passing the Crittenden-Johnson resolution affirming the purpose of the war to be preservation of the Union and not interference with the "established institutions"—that is, slavery—of the seceded states. Since those states, in the administration's theory, were still legally *in* the Union, they continued to enjoy all their constitutional rights, including slavery.

Abolitionists and radical Republicans who wanted to turn this conflict into a war to abolish slavery expressed a different theory. They maintained that by seceding and making war on the United States, southern states had forfeited their rights under the Constitution. Radicals pointed out that the blockade and the treatment of captured rebel soldiers as prisoners of war had established the belligerent status of the Confederacy as a power at war with the United States. Thus its slaves could be confiscated as enemy property. The confiscation act passed by Congress in August 1861 did authorize a limited degree of confiscation of slaves who had been employed directly in support of the Confederate war effort.

Two Union generals went even farther than this. In September 1861, John C. Frémont, commander of Union forces in the border slave state of Missouri, proclaimed martial law in the state and declared the slaves of all Confederate sympathizers free. General David Hunter did the same the following spring in the "Department of the South"—the states of South Carolina, Georgia, and Florida, where Union forces occupied a few beachheads along the coast.

Lincoln revoked both of these military edicts. He feared that they would alienate the border-state Unionists he was still cultivating. Lincoln considered the allegiance of these states crucial; he would like to have God on his side, he reportedly said, but he must have Kentucky, and Frémont's emancipation order would probably "ruin our rather fair prospect for Kentucky" if he let it stand.[22] Lincoln at this time was also trying to maintain a bipartisan coalition in the North on behalf of the war effort. Nearly half of the northern people had voted Democratic in 1860. They supported a war for the Union but many of them probably would not support a war against slavery. General McClellan, himself a Democrat as well as the North's most prominent general in 1862, warned Lincoln about this in an unsolicited letter of advice concerning national strategy in July 1862 (after the failure of his Peninsula campaign). "It should not be a war looking to the subjugation of the [southern] people," the general instructed his commander in chief. "Neither confiscation of property . . . [n]or forcible abolition of slavery should be contemplated for a moment. . . . A declaration of radical views, especially upon slavery, will rapidly disintegrate our present armies."[23]

But by this time Lincoln had begun to move precisely in the direction that McClellan advised against. He had concluded that McClellan's conservative counsel on national strategy was of a piece with the general's cautious and unsuccessful military strategy. The president had also become disillusioned with border-state Unionists. Three times in the spring and summer he had appealed to them for support of a plan of gradual, compensated emancipation in their states, to be paid for mostly by northern taxpayers. Lincoln hoped that border-state acceptance of such a plan would break the logjam on slavery and deprive the Confederacy of any hope for winning the allegiance of these states. But the border-state congressmen rejected Lincoln's appeal at about the same time that McClellan advised against an emancipation policy.

For Lincoln this was the last straw. A conservative, gradualist policy on slavery was clearly of a piece with the limited-war strategy that had governed Union policy during the first year of the war. The very evening that he learned of the border-state rejection of his gradual emancipation plan (July 12, 1862), the president made up his mind to issue an emancipation proclamation as a war measure to weaken the enemy. The next day he privately told Secretary of State Seward and Secretary of the Navy Welles of his decision. A week later he announced it formally to the cabinet. Lincoln now believed emancipation to be "a military necessity, absolutely essential to the preservation of the Union," he told them. "The slaves [are] undeniably an element of strength to those who had their service," he went on, "and we must decide whether that element should be with us or against us. . . . We must free the slaves or be ourselves subdued." Lincoln conceded that the loyal slaveholders of border states could not be expected to take the lead in a war measure against *disloyal* slaveholders. "The blow must fall first and foremost on . . . the rebels," he told the cabinet. "Having made war on the Government, they [are] subject to the incidents and calamities of war."[24]

All members of the cabinet agreed except Montgomery Blair, a former Democrat from Maryland. He protested that this radical measure would alienate the border states and northern Democrats. Lincoln replied that he had done his best to cajole the border states, but now "we must make the forward movement" without them. They would not like it but they would eventually accept it. As for the Democrats, Lincoln was done conciliating them. The best of them, like Secretary of War Stanton, had already come over to the Republicans while the rest formed an obstructive opposition whose "clubs would be used against us take what course we might." No, said Lincoln, it was time for "decisive and extensive measures. . . . We [want] the army to strike more vigorous blows. The Administration must set an example, and strike at the heart of the rebellion."[25]

We must strike at the heart of the rebellion to inspire the army to strike more vigorous blows. Here we have in a nutshell the rationale for emancipation as a military strategy of total war. It would weaken the enemy's war effort by disrupting its labor force and augment the Union war effort by converting part of that labor force to a northern asset. Lincoln adopted Seward's suggestion to postpone issuing the Proclamation until Union forces won a significant victory. After the battle of Antietam, Lincoln issued the preliminary Proclamation warning that on January 1, 1863, he would proclaim freedom for slaves in all states or portions of states then in rebellion against the United States. January 1 came, and with it the Proclamation applying to all or parts of ten southern states in which, by virtue of his war powers as commander in chief, Lincoln declared all slaves "forever free" as "a fit and necessary measure for suppressing said rebellion."[26]

Democrats bitterly opposed the Proclamation, and the war became thereafter primarily a Republican war. Some Democrats in the army also complained, and seemed ready to rally around McClellan as a symbol of the opposition. But by January 1863, McClellan was out of the army and several other Democratic generals were also soon removed or reassigned. Many other soldiers who had initially opposed emancipation also changed their minds as the scale of war continued to escalate. In January 1863 an Ohio colonel almost resigned his commission in protest against the Emancipation Proclamation; a year later he confessed that while "it goes hard" to admit he had been wrong, he now favored "doing away with the . . . accursed institution of Slavery. . . . Never hereafter will I either speak or vote in favor of Slavery; this is no hasty conclusion but a deep conviction."[27] By that time most Union soldiers likewise accepted the policy announced in the Emancipation Proclamation of recruiting black soldiers to fight for the Union. In August 1863, Lincoln maintained that "the emancipation policy, and the use of colored troops, constitute the heaviest blow yet dealt to the rebellion."[28]

Emancipation, then, became a crucial part of northern military strategy, an important means of winning the war. But if it remained merely a *means* it would not be a part of national strategy—that is, of the *purpose* for which the war was being fought. Nor would it meet the criterion that military strategy should be consistent with national strategy, for it would be inconsistent to fight a war using the weapon of emancipation to restore a Union that still contained slaves. Lincoln recognized this. Although restoration of the Union remained his first priority, the abolition of slavery became an end as well as a means, a war aim virtually inseparable from Union itself. The first step in making it so came in the Emancipation Proclamation, which Lincoln pronounced "an act of justice" as well as a military necessity. Of course the border states, along with Tennessee and small enclaves elsewhere in the Confederate states, were not covered by the Proclamation because they were under Union control and not at war with the United States and thus exempt from an executive action that could legally be based only on the president's war powers. But Lincoln kept up his pressure on the border states to adopt emancipation themselves. With his support, leaders committed to the abolition of slavery gained political power in Maryland and Missouri. They pushed through constitutional reforms that abolished slavery in those states before the end of the war.

Lincoln's presidential reconstruction policy, announced in December 1863, offered pardon and amnesty to southerners who took an oath of allegiance to the Union *and* to all wartime policies concerning slavery and emancipation. Reconstructed governments sponsored by Lincoln in Louisiana, Arkansas, and Tennessee abolished slavery in those states—at least in the portions of them controlled by Union troops—before the war ended. West Virginia came in as a new state in 1863 with a constitution pledged to abolish slavery. And in 1864, Lincoln took the lead in getting the Republican national convention that renominated him to adopt a platform calling for a Thirteenth Amendment to the Constitution prohibiting slavery everywhere in the United States. Because slavery was "hostile to the principles of republican government, justice, and national safety," declared the platform, Republicans vowed to accomplish its "utter and complete extirpation from the soil of the republic." Emancipation had thus become an end as well as a means of Union victory. As Lincoln stated in the Gettysburg Address, the North fought from 1863 on for "a new birth of freedom."[29]

Most southerners agreed with Jefferson Davis that emancipation and the northern enlistment of black soldiers were "the most execrable measures in the history of guilty man." Davis and his Congress announced an intention to execute Union officers captured in states affected by the Emancipation Proclamation as "criminals engaged in inciting servile insurrection."[30] The Confederacy did not carry out this threat, but it did return many captured black soldiers to slavery. And southern military units did, on several occasions, murder captured black soldiers and their officers instead of taking them prisoners.

Emancipation and the enlistment of slaves as soldiers tremendously increased the stakes in this war, for the South as well as the North. Southerners vowed to fight "to the last ditch" before yielding to a Yankee nation that could commit such execrable deeds. Gone was any hope of an armistice or a negotiated peace so long as the Lincoln administration was in power. The alternatives were reduced starkly to southern independence on the one hand or unconditional surrender of the South on the other.

By midsummer 1864 it looked like the former alternative—southern independence—was likely to prevail. This was one of the darkest periods of the war for the North. Its people had watched the beginning of Grant's and Sherman's military campaigns in the spring with high hopes that they would finally crush the rebellion within a month or two. But by July, Grant was bogged down before Petersburg after his army had suffered enormous casualties in a vain effort to hammer Lee into submission, while Sherman seemed similarly stymied in his attempt to capture Atlanta and break up the Confederate army defending it. War weariness and defeatism corroded the morale of northerners as they contemplated the seemingly endless cost of this war in the lives of their young men. Informal peace negotiations between Horace Greeley and Confederate agents in Canada and between two northern citizens and Jefferson Davis in Richmond during July succeeded only in eliciting the uncompromising terms of both sides. Lincoln wrote down his terms for Greeley in these words: "The restoration of the Union and abandonment of slavery." Davis made his terms equally clear: "We are fighting for INDEPENDENCE and that, or extermination, we will have."[31] As Lincoln later commented on this exchange, Davis "does not attempt to deceive us. He affords us no excuse to deceive ourselves. He cannot voluntarily reaccept the Union; we cannot voluntarily yield it. Between him and us the issue is distinct, simple, and inflexible. It is an issue which can only be tried by war, and decided by victory."[32]

This was Lincoln's most direct affirmation of unconditional surrender as the *sine qua non* of his national strategy. In it he mentioned Union as the only inflexible issue between North and South, but events in the late summer of 1864 gave Lincoln ample opportunity to demonstrate that he now considered emancipation to be an integral part of that inflexible issue of Union. Northern morale dropped to its lowest point in August. "The people are wild for peace," reported Republican political leaders. Northern Democrats were calling the war a failure and preparing to nominate McClellan on a platform demanding an armistice and peace negotiations. Democratic propagandists had somehow managed to convince their party faithful, and a good many Republicans as well, that Lincoln's insistence on coupling emancipation with Union was the only stumbling block to peace negotiations, despite Jefferson Davis's insistence that Union itself was the stumbling block. Some Republican leaders put enormous pressure on Lincoln to smoke out Davis on this issue by offering peace with Union as the only condition. To do so would, of course, give the impression of backing down on emancipation as a war aim.

These pressures filled Lincoln with dismay. The "sole purpose" of the war *was* to restore the Union, he told wavering

Republicans. "But no human power can subdue this rebellion without using the Emancipation lever as I have done." More than 100,000 black soldiers were fighting for the Union, and their efforts were crucial to northern victory. They would not continue fighting if they thought the North intended "to betray them. . . . If they stake their lives for us they must be prompted by the strongest motive . . . the promise of freedom. And the promise being made, must be kept. . . . There have been men who proposed to me to return to slavery the black warriors" who had risked their lives for the Union. "I should be damned in time & in eternity for so doing. The world shall know that I will keep my faith to friends & enemies, come what will."[33]

Nevertheless, Lincoln did waver temporarily in the face of the overwhelming pressure to drop emancipation as a precondition of peace negotiations. He drafted a private letter to a northern Democrat that included this sentence: "If Jefferson Davis wishes to know what I would do if he were to offer peace and re-union, saying nothing about slavery, let him try me." And Lincoln also drafted instructions for Henry Raymond, editor of the *New York Times* and chairman of the Republican national committee, to go to Richmond as a special envoy to propose "that upon the restoration of the Union and the national authority, the war shall cease at once, all remaining questions to be left for adjustment by peaceful modes." But Lincoln did not send the letter and he decided against sending Raymond to Richmond. Even though the president was convinced in August 1864 that he would not be re-elected, he decided that to give the appearance of backing down on emancipation "would be worse than losing the Presidential contest."[34]

In the end, of course, Lincoln achieved a triumphant re-election because northern morale revived after Sherman's capture of Atlanta and Sheridan's smashing victories in the Shenandoah Valley during September and October. Soon after the election Sherman began his devastating march from Atlanta to the sea. George Thomas's Union army in Tennessee destroyed John Bell Hood's Confederate Army of Tennessee at the battles of Franklin and Nashville. One disaster followed another for the Confederates during the winter of 1864–65, while Lincoln reiterated his determination to accept no peace short of unconditional surrender. And he left the South in no doubt of that determination. In his message to Congress on December 6, Lincoln cited statistics showing that the Union army and navy were the largest in the world, northern population was growing, and northern war production increasing. Union resources, he announced, "are unexhausted, and . . . inexhaustible. . . . We are *gaining* strength, and may, if need be, maintain the contest indefinitely."[35]

This was a chilling message to the South, whose resources were just about exhausted. Once more men of good will on both sides tried to set up peace negotiations to stop the killing. On February 3, 1865, Lincoln himself and Secretary of State Seward met with three high Confederate officials including Vice-President Alexander H. Stephens on board a Union ship anchored at Hampton Roads, Virginia. During four hours of talks Lincoln budged not an inch from his minimum conditions for peace, which he described as: "1) The restoration of the National authority throughout all the states. 2) No receding by the Executive of the United States on the Slavery question. 3) No cessation of hostilities short of an end of the war, and the disbanding of all forces hostile to the government." The Confederate commissioners returned home empty-handed, angry because they considered these terms "nothing less than unconditional surrender."[36] Of course they were, but Lincoln had never during the past two years given the South reason to expect anything else.

Lincoln returned to Washington to prepare his second inaugural address, which ranks in its eloquence and its evocation of the meaning of this war with the Gettysburg Address itself. Reviewing the past four years, Lincoln admitted that neither side had "expected for the war, the magnitude, or the duration, which it has already achieved. Each looked for an easier triumph, and a result less fundamental and astounding." Back in the days when the North looked for an easier triumph, Lincoln might have added, he had pursued a national strategy of limited war to restore the *status quo ante bellum*. But when the chances of an easy triumph disappeared, Lincoln grasped the necessity for a strategy of total war to overthrow the enemy's social and political system.

Whatever flaws historians might find in Lincoln's military strategy, it is hard to find fault with his national strategy. His sense of timing and his sensitivity to the pulse of the northern people were superb. As he once told a visiting delegation of abolitionists, if he had issued the Emancipation Proclamation six months sooner than he did, "public sentiment would not have sustained it."[37] He might have added that if he had waited six months longer, it would have come too late. After skillfully steering a course between proslavery Democrats and antislavery Republicans during the first eighteen months of war, Lincoln guided a new majority coalition of Republicans and converted Democrats through the uncharted waters of total war and emancipation filled with sharp reefs and rocks, emerging triumphant into a second term on a platform of unconditional surrender that gave the nation a new birth of freedom.

V How Lincoln Won the War
with Metaphors

In an essay on the reasons for Confederate defeat in the Civil War, southern historian David M. Potter made a striking assertion: "If the Union and Confederacy had exchanged presidents with one another, the Confederacy might have won its independence." Is this rather dramatic conclusion justified? Most historians would probably agree with Potter's general point that Davis's shortcomings as a leader played a role in Confederate defeat. They would also agree that one of Davis's principal failures was an inability to communicate effectively with other Confederate leaders and with the southern people. As Potter put it, Davis "seemed to think in abstractions and to speak in platitudes."[1]

Lincoln, by contrast, most emphatically did *not* think in abstractions and rarely spoke in platitudes. We have not had another president—except perhaps Franklin D. Roosevelt—who expressed himself in such a clear, forceful, logical manner as Lincoln. It is no coincidence that Lincoln and Roosevelt were great war presidents who led the United States to its most decisive victories in its most important wars. Their pre-eminent quality as leaders was an ability to communicate the meaning and purpose of these wars in an intelligible, inspiring manner that helped energize and mobilize their people to make the sacrifices necessary for victory. By contrast, Jefferson Davis, as another historian has concluded, failed to do a good job "in eliciting the enthusiasm and energies of the people."[2]

Wherein lay Lincoln's advantage over Davis in this matter? It certainly did not derive from a better education. Davis had received one of the best educations that money could buy in his day. He attended one "college" in Kentucky and another in Mississippi, which were really secondary schools or academies; he went to Transylvania University in Kentucky, which was one of the best genuine colleges west of the Appalachians at that time; and he graduated from the military academy at West Point, the best American school for engineering as well as for military science in that era. From his education Davis acquired excellent training in the classics, in rhetoric, logic, literature, and science. He should have been a superb communicator. And in many respects he was, by the standards of the time. He could write with vigorous logic, turn a classical phrase, quote the leading authorities on many a subject, and close with a rhetorical flourish.

Lincoln had only a year or so of formal schooling in the typical rote-learning "blab schools" of the day, schooling that he obtained, as he later put it, "by littles"—a month here, a couple of months there, spread out over a period of a few years. Lincoln was basically a self-taught man. Of course he later read law, which along with the practice of that profession helped to give him an ability to write and speak with clarity, a skill in logical analysis, and a knack for finding exactly the right word or phrase to express his meaning. But Jefferson Davis also possessed most of these skills of expository writing and speaking. So we are still left with the question: wherein lay Lincoln's superiority?

The answer may be found in a paradox: perhaps the defects of Lincoln's education proved a benefit. Instead of spending years inside the four walls of a classroom, Lincoln worked on frontier dirt farms most of his youth, he split rails, he rafted down the Mississippi on a flatboat, he surveyed land, he worked in a store where he learned to communicate with the farmers and other residents of a rural community. Lincoln grew up close to the rhythms of nature, of wild beasts and farm animals, of forest and running water, of seasons and crops and of people who got their meager living from the land. These things, more than books, furnished his earliest education. They infused his speech with the images of nature. And when he turned to books, what were his favorites? They were the King James Bible, *Aesop's Fables, Pilgrim's Progress,* and Shakespeare's plays. What do these four have in common? They are rich in figurative language—in allegory, parable, fable, metaphor—in words and stories that seem to say one thing but mean another, in images that illustrate something more profound than their surface appearance.

Here lies one of the secrets of Lincoln's success as a communicator: his skill in the use of figurative language, of which metaphor is the most common example. We all use metaphors every day. We tell someone to stop beating around the bush; we say that we have too many irons in the fire; we express a desire to get to the heart of the matter; we worry about fitting square pegs in round holes; we see light at the end of the tunnel; and so on. Most of these examples are "dead" metaphors—that is, they are so commonplace that we often do not realize that we *are* metaphors, and they thus lose their power to evoke a vivid image in our minds. The best "live" metaphors are those that use a simple, concrete figure to illustrate a complex and perhaps abstract concept, thereby giving life and tangible meaning to something that might otherwise escape comprehension.

One of the first things that strikes a student of Lincoln's speeches and writings is his frequent use of images and figurative language. His speeches and letters abound with metaphors. Many of them are extraordinarily well chosen and apt; they have the persuasive power of concreteness and clarity. By contrast, Jefferson Davis's prose contains few metaphors or images of any kind. It is relentlessly literal. It is formal, precise, logical, but also stiff, cold, and abstract. Davis's wartime letters and speeches bristle with anger and bitterness toward Yankees and toward Davis's critics and adversaries within the Confederacy. But the few metaphors he used to illustrate his points are quite dead—references to sowing the seeds of discontent and thereby harvesting defeat, and the like.

To be sure, a number of Lincoln's metaphors were dead on arrival. He complained of dealing with people who had axes to grind; he said more than once that he wanted everyone to have a fair start in the race of life; he referred to the ship of state and its navigational problems during his presidency; and so on. But Lincoln could neatly turn a seemingly dead metaphor into a live one. In his first message to a special session of Congress that met three months after the war began, Lincoln critically reviewed the long and, as he put it, sophistic attempt by southern leaders to legitimize their actions by arguments for state sovereignty and the constitutional right of secession. "With rebellion thus sugar-coated," said the president, "they have been drugging the public mind of their section for more than thirty years," and this war was the result. Here Lincoln injected life into a rather tired metaphor, "sugar-coated," and used it to clinch his point in a luminous manner. This occasion also gave Lincoln an opportunity to define his philosophy of communication with the public. When the government printer set the message in type he objected to the phrase about sugar-coating the rebellion. "You have used an undignified expression in the message," the printer told the president. "A message to Congress [is] a different affair from a speech at a mass-meeting in Illinois. . . . The messages [become] a part of history, and should be written accordingly. . . . I would alter the structure of that, if I were you." Lincoln replied with a twinkle in his eye: "That word expresses precisely my idea, and I am not going to change it. The time will never come in this country when the people won't know exactly what *sugar-coated* means!"[3] Lincoln was right; people knew exactly what he meant then, and his metaphor retains its pithiness today.

Lincoln used a different but equally expressive metaphor to describe the threat of secession on another important occasion, his speech at Cooper Institute in New York in February 1860, a speech that gave him great visibility among eastern Republicans and helped launch him toward the presidential nomination three months later. This time he discussed southern warnings to the North of the dire consequences if a Republican president was elected. "In that supposed event," said Lincoln directing his words to the South, "you say, you will destroy the Union; and then, you say, the great crime of having destroyed it will be upon us! That is cool. A highwayman holds a pistol to my ear, and mutters through his teeth, 'Stand and deliver, or I shall kill you, and then you will be a murderer!'"[4]

No one could fail to understand Lincoln's point. And through his whole life one of his main concerns was that everyone understand precisely what he was saying. A colleague who praised this quality once asked Lincoln where his concern with exact clarity came from. "Among my earliest recollections," replied Lincoln, "I remember how, when a mere child, I used to get irritated when anybody talked to me in a way I could not understand. I don't think I ever got angry at anything else in my life. . . . I can remember going to my little bedroom, after hearing the neighbors talk of an evening with my father, and spending the night walking up and down, and trying to make out what was the exact meaning of some of their, to me, dark sayings. I could not sleep . . . when I got on such a hunt after an idea, until I had caught it; and when I thought I had got it, I was not satisfied . . . until I had put it in language plain enough, as I thought, for any boy I knew to comprehend. This was a kind of passion with me, and it has stuck by me."[5]

Many contemporaries testified to this Lincolnian passion, and to his genius for using everyday metaphors to achieve it. Francis Carpenter, the artist who spent six months at the White House during 1864 painting a picture of Lincoln and his cabinet, noted that the president's "lightest as well as his most powerful thought almost invariably took on the form of a figure of speech, which drove the point *home*, and *clinched* it, as few abstract reasoners are able to do." Lincoln was also famous for tellling stories. Many of them were parables intended to make or illustrate a point; and a parable is an extended metaphor. "It is not the story itself," Lincoln once said, "but its purpose, or effect, that interests me."[6]

When Lincoln said, "Now that reminds me of a story," his listeners knew that they could expect a parable. Take for example this story that Lincoln told soon after he had gotten rid of his controversial Secretary of War Simon Cameron. Since some other cabinet members had also made enemies among one faction or another, a delegation of politicians called on the president and advised him that this might be a good time to make a wholesale change in the cabinet. Lincoln shook his head and replied, "This reminds me of a story. When I was a boy I knew a farmer named Joe Wilson who was proud of his prize chickens. But he started to lose some of them to raids by skunks on the henhouse. One night he heard a loud cackling from the chickens and crept out with his shotgun to find a half-dozen of the black and white critters running in and out of the shed. Thinking to clean out the whole tribe, he put a double charge in the gun and fired away. Somehow he hit only one, and the rest scampered off." At this point in the story, Lincoln would act it out by holding his nose and screwing up his face in a pained expression, while he continued. "The neighbors asked Joe why he didn't follow up the skunks and kill the rest. 'Blast it,' said Joe, 'it was eleven weeks before I got over killin' *one*. If you want any more skirmishing in that line you can just do it yourselves!' "[7]

Nobody could fail to get Lincoln's point. But not everyone approved of his habit of telling stories—some of which were a good bit more earthy than this one. Some people considered it undignified for the president of the United States to carry on in such a fashion. But Lincoln had a reply for them, as related by Chauncey Depew, a prominent lawyer, railroad president, and New York Republican leader. "I heard him tell a great many stories," said Depew, "many of which would not do exactly for the drawing room, but for the person he wished to reach, and the object he desired to accomplish with the individual, the story did more than any argument could have done. He once said to me, in reference to some sharp criticism which had been made upon his story-telling: . . . 'I have found in the course of a long experience that common people'—and, repeating it—'common people, take them as they run, are more easily influenced and informed through the medium of a broad illustration than in any other way, and as to what the hypercritical few may think, I don't care.' "[8]

This was something that Jefferson Davis never understood. He would never be caught telling a story about skunks to make a point about political timing and leadership. He did not have Lincoln's concern for reaching the common people or his knack for doing so. Lincoln was especially fond of animal metaphors and parables, as in the case of the skunk story. This derived in part from his own rural background. It also undoubtedly derived from the many boyhood hours he spent with *Aesop's Fables*. During one of those hours his cousin Dennis Hanks said to him: "Abe, them yarns is all lies." Lincoln looked up for a moment, and replied: "Mighty darn good lies, Denny."[9] And as an adult Lincoln knew that these "lies," these fables about animals, provided an excellent way to communicate with a people who were still close to their rural roots and understood the idioms of the forest and barnyard.

Some of Lincoln's most piquant animal metaphors occurred in his comments about or communications with commanding generals during the war. General George B. McClellan clamored repeatedly for reinforcements and understated his own strength while overstating that of the enemy. On one of these occasions Lincoln, who had already reinforced McClellan and knew that Union forces outnumbered the Confederates, said in exasperation that sending troops to McClellan was like shoveling flies across the barnyard—most of them never seemed to get there. Later on, when Joseph Hooker had become commander of the Army of the Potomac, Lincoln visited him at the front. Hooker boasted that he had built this force into "the finest army on the planet." He added that he hoped God Almighty would have mercy on Bobby Lee because he, Joe Hooker, would have none. Lincoln listened to this and commented that "the hen is the wisest of all the animal creation because she never cackles until the egg is laid."[10] And to be sure, it was Lee who laid the egg by beating Hooker decisively at Chancellorsville. Lee then invaded the North in the campaign that led to Gettysburg. As Lee began to move north, Hooker proposed to cross the Rappahannock River and attack his rear guard. Lincoln disapproved with these words in a telegram to Hooker: "I would not take any risk of being entangled upon the river, like an ox jumped half over a fence, and liable to be torn by dogs, front and rear, without a fair chance to gore one way or kick the other." Napoleon himself could not have given better tactical advice or phrased it half so well. A week later, when the Confederate invasion force was strung out over nearly a hundred miles of Virginia roads, Lincoln telegraphed Hooker: "If the head of Lee's army is at Martinsburg and the tail of it on the Plank road between Fredericksburg and Chancellorsville, the animal must be very slim somewhere. Could you not break him?"[11] But Hooker seemed reluctant to fight Lee again, so Lincoln replaced him with George G. Meade who won the battle of Gettysburg but proved to be cautious and defensive afterward.

Thus in 1864 Lincoln brought to the East his most successful commander, Ulysses S. Grant, to become general in chief. In a private conference with Grant soon after he arrived in Washington, Lincoln referred to the military situation and told Grant he could best illustrate what he wanted to say by a story. There was once a great war among the animals, said the president, and one side had great diffculty finding a commander who had enough confidence in himself to fight. Finally they found a monkey, by the name of Jocko, who said he could command the army if his tail could be made a little longer. So the other animals found more tail and spliced it onto Jocko's. He looked at it admiringly, but said he thought he needed just a little more. So they found some more and spliced it on. This process was repeated many times until Jocko's tail was so long that when coiled it filled the whole room. Still he called for more tail, and they kept adding by coiling it around his shoulders and then around his whole body until he suffocated. Grant understood the point; unlike McClellan and other generals, he would not keep calling for more troops as an excuse for not fighting.[12]

Instead, the new general in chief worked out a plan for the two main Union armies, in Virginia and Georgia, to advance simultaneously against the two principal Confederate armies while smaller Union forces elsewhere pinned down

Confederate detachments to prevent them from reinforcing the main armies. This was the kind of coordinated offensive that Lincoln had been urging on his generals for two years, and he was delighted finally to have a commander who would do it. Lincoln's expressive description of the auxiliary role of the smaller armies on the periphery was: "Those not skinning can hold a leg."[13] Grant liked this phrase so much that he used it in his own dispatches.

Later on, when Grant had Lee's army under siege at Petersburg while Sherman was marching through Georgia and South Carolina destroying everything in his path, Lincoln described Union strategy in this fashion: "Grant has the bear by the hind leg while Sherman takes off the hide." On another occasion Lincoln changed the metaphor in an official telegram to Grant: "I have seen your despatch expressing your unwillingness to break your hold where you are. Neither am I willing. Hold on with a bull-dog grip, and chew & choke, as much as possible."[14] In the end it was Grant's chewing and choking while Sherman took off the hide that won the war.

The principal cause of this war was slavery and one of its main consequences was the abolition of slavery. This peculiar institution gave rise to many Lincolnian metaphors, animal and otherwise. One of them was a metaphor of snakes and children that Lincoln used in several speeches during his tour of New England in the late winter of 1860. The central tenet of the Republican party's policy was to restrict the spread of slavery into new territories while pledging not to interfere with it in states where it already existed and was therefore protected by the Constitution. Lincoln considered slavery a moral wrong and a social evil. He hoped that the South would eventually take steps to end it voluntarily and peacefully. In the meantime, he said, we must not introduce this evil where it does not now exist. "If I saw a venomous snake crawling in the road," said Lincoln in illustration of his point, "any man would say I might seize the nearest stick and kill it; but if I found that snake in bed with my children, that would be another question. I might hurt the children more than the snake, and it might bite them. . . . But if there was a bed newly made up, to which the children were to be taken, and it was proposed to take a batch of young snakes and put them there with them, I take it no man would say there was any question how I ought to decide. . . . The new Territories are the newly made bed to which our children are to go, and it lies with the nation to say whether they shall have snakes mixed up with them or not."[15]

In our day of 30-second political spot commercials on television, this metaphor seems long and involved. But Lincoln's audiences understood it perfectly and appreciated it boisterously. The stenographic report of this speech at New Haven indicates prolonged applause, laughter, and cheering as he spun out the metaphor. A professor of rhetoric at Yale was so taken with Lincoln's speech that he followed him to another town to hear him speak again and then gave a lecture on Lincoln's techniques to his class. After Lincoln spoke at Norwich, Connecticut, the town's leading clergyman happened to travel on the same train with Lincoln next day and talked with him, praising his style, "especially your illustrations, which were romance and pathos, and fun and logic all welded together. That story about the snakes, for example . . . was at once queer and comical, and tragic and argumentative. It broke through all the barriers of a man's previous opinions and prejudices at a crash, and blew up the citadel of his false theories before he could know what had hurt him."[16]

Lincoln used a number of other metaphors to describe slavery, including that of a cancer which must be prevented from spreading lest it kill the body politic. His best-known slavery metaphor formed the central theme of the most famous speech he gave before the Civil War, the House Divided address in 1858. Here the house was a metaphor for the Union, which had been divided against itself by slavery and could not continue to be so divided forever without collapsing. Therefore the Republicans wanted to stop the further spread of slavery as a first step toward what Lincoln called its "ultimate extinction." This metaphor of a house divided became probably the single most important image of the relationship between slavery and the Union, and remains so today. It provided an instant mental picture of what Republicans stood for. It also helped provoke the South into secession when Lincoln was elected president, because no matter how much Lincoln professed his intention to tolerate slavery where it already existed, had not this Black Republican Yankee also called slavery a moral wrong and looked forward to its ultimate extinction?

In that same speech, Lincoln elaborated the house metaphor to illustrate another of the Republican party's favorite themes—that the Democrats were dominated by a "slave power conspiracy" to expand the institution of bondage over the whole country. "When we see a lot of framed timbers," said Lincoln, "different portions of which we know have been gotten out at different times and places by different workmen—Stephen, Franklin, Roger and James, for instance—and when we see these timbers joined together, and see they exactly make the frame of a house . . . we find it impossible not to *believe* that Stephen and Franklin and Roger and James all understood one another from the beginning, and all worked upon a common *plan* or *draft*."[17] The point of this rather elaborate metaphor seems obscure today. But Lincoln's audience knew exactly what he was talking about. The four men he named were Stephen Douglas, leader of the Democratic party, Franklin Pierce and James Buchanan, the previous and current presidents of the United States, both Democrats, and Roger Taney, chief justice of the Supreme Court, also a Democrat. The house for which each of them separately framed timbers, but with a secret understanding to make everything fit together, was a conspiracy to expand slavery. The timbers were the Kansas-Nebraska Act that repealed the Missouri Compromise and made possible the expansion of slavery north of latitude 36° 30′ where it had previously been prohibited; the Dred Scott decision that legalized slavery in all territories; the Democratic pledge to acquire Cuba as a new slave territory; and other items.

After the Civil War broke out, Lincoln's main problem— next to winning the war—was what to do about slavery. And by the second year of war the slavery issue became bound up with the fate of the Union itself as Lincoln gradually came to the conclusion that he could not win the war without striking down slavery.

In his public and private communications concerning slavery during the war, Lincoln used a number of telling metaphors and similes. His first effort was to persuade the loyal border states to accept a policy of gradual, compensated emancipation. This proposal, he said in an appeal to the people of the border states in May 1862, "makes common cause for a common object, casting no reproaches on any. It acts not the pharisee. The change it contemplates would come gently as the dews of heaven, not rending or wrecking anything. Will you not embrace it?" When the border states did not respond, Lincoln shifted from soft blandishment to blunt warning. In July 1862 he called border-state congressmen to the White House. By then the war had taken a harder turn. Republican congressmen had passed a bill to confiscate the property of rebels against the government, including their slave property. Lincoln himself had just about decided to issue an emancipation proclamation to apply to the Confederate states. The impact of these measures was bound to spill over into the Unionist border states. Slaves there were already emancipating themselves by running away to Union army lines. In these circumstances Lincoln now told border-state congressmen that his plan of gradual emancipation with compensation from the federal government was the best they could get. Otherwise, as the war continued to escalate in intensity, "the institution in your states will be extinguished by mere friction and abrasion."[18] The image of friction and abrasion was a most appropriate one, but it left the border-state congressmen unmoved. Most of them voted against Lincoln's offer—and three more years of war did extinguish slavery by friction and abrasion, in the border states as well as in the Confederate states.

After his unsuccessful appeal to the border states, Lincoln made up his mind to issue an emancipation proclamation. He used a variety of metaphors to explain his reasons for doing so. "It had got to midsummer 1862," the president later summarized. "Things had gone on from bad to worse, until I felt that we had reached the end of our rope on the plan of operations we had been pursuing; that we had about played our last card, and must change our tactics, or lose the game!"[19] Both metaphors here—the end of our rope and played our last card—are rather tired, almost dead, but nevertheless the context and the importance of the issue bring them alive and make them work. Lincoln liked the card-playing metaphor; in letters to conservatives who objected to the government's total-war policy of confiscation and emancipation, Lincoln wrote with some asperity that "this government cannot much longer play a game in which it stakes all, and its enemies stake nothing. . . . It may as well be understood, once for all, that I shall not surrender this game leaving any available card unplayed."[20]

Lincoln used other, more original and expressive metaphors at the same time, asking one conservative if he expected the government to wage this war "with elder-stalk squirts, charged with rose water." To a southern Unionist who had complained that emancipation of slaves owned by rebels would inevitably expand into emancipation of slaves owned by loyal Unionists as well, Lincoln replied with an angry letter denouncing those Unionists who did nothing to help the North win the war and who expected the government to take time out to protect their property while it was struggling for its very survival. The president spun out a metaphor of a ship in a storm to clinch the point. Do southern Unionists expect, he asked, "to touch neither a sail nor a pump, but to be merely passengers,—deadheads at that—to be carried snug and dry, throughout the storm, and safely landed right side up[?] Nay, more; even a mutineer is to go untouched lest these sacred passengers receive an accidental wound."[21]

When the constitutionality of the emancipation proclamation was questioned, Lincoln defended it not only by citing his military powers as commander in chief in time of war to seize enemy property, but he also used an apt metaphor to illustrate how a lesser constitutional right—of property in slaves—might have to be sacrificed in the interests of a greater constitutional duty—that of preserving the nation's life. "Often a limb must be amputated to save a life," Lincoln pointed out in this age without antibiotics when everyone knew of wounded soldiers who had lost an arm or leg to stop the spread of fatal infections. "The surgeon," Lincoln continued, "is solemnly bound to try to save both life *and* limb; but when the crisis comes, and the limb must be sacrificed as the only chance of saving the life, no honest man will hesitate. . . . In our case, the moment came when I felt that slavery must die that the nation might live!"[22]

One final metaphor that Lincoln used to illustrate a point about slavery is particularly striking. This one concerned the definition of liberty. The South professed to have seceded and gone to war in defense of its rights and liberties. The chief liberty that southerners believed to be threatened by the election of Lincoln was their right to own slaves. In a public speech in 1864 at Baltimore, in a border state where the frictions and abrasions of war had by then just about ground up slavery, Lincoln illustrated the paradox of conflicting definitions of liberty with an Aesopian fable. "The shepherd drives the wolf from the sheep's throat, for which the sheep thanks the shepherd as a *liberator,* while the wolf denounces him for the same act as a destroyer of liberty, especially as the sheep was a black one."[23] This image leaves no doubt which definition of liberty Lincoln subscribed to, or whose cause in this war—the northern shepherd's or the southern wolf's—was the nobler one. This passage comes as close to a lyrical expression of northern purpose as anything short of poetry could.

And at times Lincoln's words became poetic. He liked to read poetry. His favorites were Burns, Byron, and above all Shakespeare. He knew much of Burns and Shakespeare by heart. As president, Lincoln liked to relax by going to the theater—as we know to our sorrow. He went to every play of Shakespeare's that came to Washington. He especially enjoyed reading the tragedies and historical plays with a political theme. The quintessence of poetry is imagery, particularly metaphor, and this is true most of all for Shakespeare's plays. Lincoln's fondness for this medium undoubtedly helped shape his use of figurative and symbolic language. As a youth he had tried his hand at writing poetry. But the way in which we best know Lincoln as a poet is through several famous passages from his wartime speeches and state papers, in which he achieved unrivaled eloquence through the use of poetic language.

A rather modest example of this occurs in a public letter that Lincoln wrote in August 1863 to be read at a Union rally in Illinois—and of course to be published in the newspapers. This letter came at a major turning point in the war. Union armies had recently captured Vicksburg and won the battle of Gettysburg, reversing a year of defeats that had created vitiating doubt and dissent. But even after these victories the antiwar Copperhead movement remained strong and threatening. Its animus focused mainly on the government's policy of emancipation and the enlistment of black troops. By the time of Lincoln's letter, several black regiments had already demonstrated their mettle in combat. Lincoln addressed all of these issues. In delightful and easily understood imagery he noted the importance of the capture of Vicksburg in opening the Mississippi River and gave credit to soldiers and sailors of all regions, including black soldiers and loyal southern whites, in accomplishing this result. "The signs look better," wrote the president. "The Father of Waters again goes unvexed to the sea. Thanks to the great North-West for it. Nor yet wholly to them. Three hundred miles up, they met New-England, Empire, Key-Stone, and Jersey, hewing their way right and left. The Sunny South too, in more colors than one, also lent a hand. On the spot, their part of the history was jotted down in black and white. . . . Nor must Uncle Sam's Web-feet be forgotten. . . . Not only on the deep sea, the broad bay, and the rapid river, but also up the narrow muddy bayou, wherever the ground was a little damp, they have been, and made their tracks." Shifting from these cheerful, almost playful images, Lincoln turned to the Copperheads who had been denigrating emancipation and calling the whole war effort a useless and wicked failure. It was not a failure, said Lincoln; the Union had turned the corner toward victory. And when that victory came, "there will be some black men who can remember that, with silent tongue, and clenched teeth, and steady eye, and well-poised bayonet, they have helped mankind on to this great consummation; while, I fear, there will be some white ones, unable to forget that, with malignant heart, and deceitful speech, they have strove to hinder it."[24]

Here Lincoln was writing primarily about a *process*—about

the means of victory in the war for the Union. It was when he defined the *purpose* of that war—the meaning of Union and why it was worth fighting for—that he soared to his greatest poetic eloquence. "Union" was something of an abstraction that required concrete symbols to make its meaning clear to the people who would have to risk their lives for it. The flag was the most important such symbol. But Lincoln wanted to go beyond the flag and strike deeper symbolic chords of patriotism. And in so doing he furnished some of the finest examples of poetic metaphor in our national literature.

In the peroration of his first inaugural address, Lincoln appealed to the South with an evocation of the symbols of a common history and shared memories as metaphors for the Union. "We must not be enemies," he declared. "Though passion may have strained, it must not break our bonds of affection. The mystic chords of memory, stretching from every battle-field, and patriot grave, to every living heart and hearthstone, all over this broad land, will yet swell the chorus of the Union, when again touched, as surely they will be, by the better angels of our nature."[25]

Having here summoned forth the past as a metaphor for Union, Lincoln invoked the future in the peroration of his message to Congress in December 1862. Now he added emancipation to Union as the legacy which the people of that generation would leave to their children's children. "Fellow-citizens, *we* cannot escape history. . . . The fiery trial through which we pass, will light us down, in honor or dishonor, to the latest generation. . . . We shall nobly save, or meanly lose, the last best, hope of earth. . . . In *giving* freedom to the *slave*, we *assure* freedom to the *free*."[26]

Lincoln put these symbolic themes of past, present, and future together in the most famous of his poems, the Gettysburg Address. In this elegy there are no metaphors in a conventional sense; rather there are what two literary scholars have called "concealed" or "structural" metaphors—that is, metaphors that are built into the structure of the address in such a way that they are not visible but are essential to its meaning.[27] The Gettysburg Address contains three parallel sets of three images each that are intricately interwoven: past, present, future; continent, nation, battlefield; and birth, death, rebirth. Let us disaggregate these metaphors for purposes of analysis, even though in the process we destroy their poetic qualities. Four score and seven years in the *past* our fathers *conceived* and *brought forth* on this *continent* a *nation* that stood for something important in the world: the proposition that all men are created equal. *Now*, our generation faces a great war testing whether such a nation standing for such an ideal can survive. In dedicating the cemetery on this *battlefield*, the living must take inspiration to finish the task that those who lie buried here nobly advanced by giving the last full measure of their devotion. Life and death in this passage have a paradoxical but metaphorical relationship: men died that the nation might live, yet metaphorically the old Union also died, and with it died the institution of slavery. After these deaths, the nation must have a "new birth of freedom" so that the government of, by, and for the people that our fathers conceived and brought forth in the past "shall not perish from the earth" but be preserved as a legacy for the *future*.[28]

Contrary to common impression, Lincoln's Gettysburg Address was not ignored or unappreciated at the time. Lincoln himself may have contributed to this legend, for he reportedly told his friend and bodyguard, Ward Hill Lamon, that the speech was "a flat failure." Mixing a live metaphor with a dead simile (as Lamon remembered it a quarter-century later), Lincoln said that the address "won't scour"; it "fell upon the audience like a wet blanket."[29] It is true that admiration for the Gettysburg Address grew over the years.

But many auditors and readers immediately recognized its greatness; one of them was Edward Everett, the main orator of the day, who wrote to Lincoln the next day: "I should be glad, if I could flatter myself, that I came as near to the central idea of the occasion, in two hours, as you did in two minutes."[30]

Jefferson Davis did not—and probably could not—write anything like the Gettysburg Address, or like anything else in the way of images and metaphors that Lincoln used to illustrate his points both great and small. Communication and inspiration are two of the most important functions of a president in times of crisis. Thus perhaps David Potter's suggestion that if the Union and Confederacy had exchanged presidents the South might have won the Civil War does not seem so farfetched after all.

VI   The Hedgehog and the Foxes

To many readers the title of this essay may seem whimsical if not obscure. "Lincoln a hedgehog?!" remarked the baffled president of the Abraham Lincoln Association when he first heard the proposed title. Lincoln himself might have appreciated the analogy—given his penchant for animal metaphors and his fondness for *Aesop's Fables*. This particular analogy might at first glance appear to be unflattering, though: the *Encyclopedia Britannica* says of the hedgehog that "the brain is remarkable for its low development." Like its larger American cousin the porcupine, the hedgehog's distinguishing characteristic is self-defense by its sharp spines, or quills.

But the notion of comparing Lincoln to a hedgehog was suggested by a line from the Greek poet Archilochus: "The fox knows many things, but the hedgehog knows one big thing." Classical scholars have disagreed about the purport of this adage. It may mean nothing more than that the fox, despite his cleverness, cannot overcome the hedgehog's one defense. But in a famous essay on Leo Tolstoy with the similar title of "The Hedgehog and the Fox," British philosopher Isaiah Berlin has provided a more profound rendering of Archilochus' words. The hedgehog is a thinker or leader who "relate[s] everything to a single central vision . . . a single, universal, organizing principle," writes Berlin, while the fox "pursue[s] many ends, often unrelated and even contradictory."[1]

In this sense, Abraham Lincoln can be considered one of the foremost hedgehogs in American history. More than any of his Civil War contemporaries, he pursued policies that were governed by a central vision, expressed in the Gettysburg Address, that this "nation, conceived in Liberty, and dedicated to the proposition that all men are created equal . . . shall not perish from the earth." Lincoln was surrounded by foxes who considered themselves smarter than he but who lacked his depth of vision and therefore sometimes pursued unrelated and contradictory ends. Two of the most prominent foxes were William H. Seward and Horace Greeley. Both were more clever than Lincoln, more nimble-witted and brilliant in conversation. They shared Lincoln's nationalism and his abhorrence of slavery. But while Lincoln navigated by the lodestar that never moved, Seward and Greeley steered by stars that constantly changed position. If they had been at the helm instead of Lincoln, it is quite likely that the United States would have foundered on the rocks of disunion.

Several of Lincoln's associates testified to the slow but tenacious qualities of his mind. Greeley himself noted that Lincoln's intellect worked "not quickly nor brilliantly, but exhaustively." A fellow lawyer in antebellum years said that in analyzing a case, writing a letter, preparing a speech, or making a decision Lincoln was "slow, calculating, methodical, and accurate."[2] The volatile William Herndon sometimes showed impatience with his partner's deliberate manner of researching or arguing a case, but conceded that while Lincoln "thought slowly and acted slowly," he "not only went to the root of the question, but dug up the root, and separated and analyzed every fibre of it." In a legal case or a political debate, recalled Leonard Swett, Lincoln would concede non-essential points to his opponent, lulling him into a false sense of complacency. "But giving away six points and carrying the seventh he carried his case . . . the whole case hanging on the seventh. . . . Any man who took Lincoln for a simple-minded man would wind up with his back in a ditch."[3]

During the war Lincoln expressed this hedgehog philosophy of concentrating on the one big thing, to the exclusion of non-essentials, in a speech to an Ohio regiment. "No small matter should divert us from our great purpose. . . . [Do not] let your minds be carried off from the great work we have before us."[4] Herndon told a story that illustrated Lincoln's remarkable capacity to focus on what he considered the essentials of any matter. Herndon visited Niagara Falls some time after Lincoln had seen the Falls in 1849. Telling Lincoln his impressions of this wonder of nature, Herndon waxed eloquent in typical nineteenth-century romantic fashion, declaiming of rush and roar and brilliant rainbows. Exhausting his adjectives, he asked Lincoln what had made the deepest impression on him when he saw the Falls. "The thing that struck me most forcibly," Lincoln replied, "was, where in the world did all that water come from?" Herndon recalled this remark after nearly forty years as an example of how Lincoln "looked at everything. . . . His mind, heedless of beauty or awe, followed irresistibly back to the first cause. . . . If there was any secret in his power this surely was it."[5]

The "first cause," the central vision that guided Lincoln the hedgehog, was preservation of the United States and its constitutional government, which he was convinced would be destroyed if the Confederate States established their independence. Lincoln's nationalism was profound. It was not merely chauvinism, not the spread-eagle jingoism typical of American oratory in the nineteenth century. It was rooted in the Declaration of Independence and the ideals of liberty and equal opportunity that the Declaration had implanted as a revolutionary new idea on which the United States was founded. One of the first books he had read as a boy, Lincoln told the New Jersey Senate in Trenton on February 21, 1861, was Parson Weems's *Life of Washington*. Nothing in that book fixed itself more vividly in his mind than the story of the Revolutionary army crossing the ice-choked Delaware River in a driving sleet storm on Christmas night 1776, at a low point in the American cause, to attack the British garrison at Trenton. "I recollect thinking then, boy even though I was, that there must have been something more than common that those men struggled for . . . something even more than National Independence . . . something that held out a great promise to all the people of the world for all time to come." This it was, said Lincoln next day at Independence Hall in Philadelphia, "which gave promise that in due time the weights should be lifted from the shoulders of all men, and that *all* should have an equal chance."[6]

On the eve of taking the oath as president of a nation that seemed to be breaking apart, Lincoln was "exceedingly anxious that this Union, the Constitution, and the liberties of the people shall be perpetuated in accordance with the original idea for which that struggle was made." Three weeks after calling out the militia to suppress the insurrection that began at Fort Sumter, Lincoln told his private secretary John Hay that "the central idea pervading this struggle" was the necessity "of proving that popular government is not an absurdity." If in a free government "the minority have the right to break up the government whenever they choose," it would "go far to prove the incapability of the people to govern themselves."[7] On July 4, 1861, Lincoln said that "our popular government has often been called an experiment." Confederate success would destroy that experiment, warned Lincoln on this and other occasions, would seal the doom of that "last best, hope" for "maintaining in the world . . . government of the people, by the people, for the people."[8]

This was the fixed and unmoving North Star by which Lincoln charted his course through the Civil War when foxes seemed to navigate by the revolving planets. During the secession winter of 1860–61, several Republican spokesmen, fearing another proslavery compromise to keep slave states in the Union, expressed a preference for letting them go in peace. "If the Cotton States shall become satisfied that they can do better out of the Union than in it, we insist on letting them go," wrote Horace Greeley in his powerful *New York Tribune*. "We hope never to live in a republic whereof one section is pinned to the residue by bayonets."[9] Whether Greeley really meant this, or hedged it around with so many qualifications and reservations as to make it meaningless, has been the subject of debate among historians. Whatever the mercurial Greeley meant, many of his contemporaries including Lincoln seem to have read his Go-in-Peace editorials literally. Lincoln complained of the *Tribune*'s "damaging vagaries about peaceable secession." Greeley wrote to the president-elect in December 1860 that what he most feared was "another disgraceful back-down of the free States. . . . Let the Union slide—it may be reconstructed. . . . But another nasty compromise, whereby everything is conceded and nothing secured, will so thoroughly disgrace and humiliate us that we can never raise our heads."[10]

"Let the Union slide—it may be reconstructed" is the language of the fox. Lincoln the hedgehog knew better. Once the principle of secession was recognized, the Union could never be restored. The United States would cease to exist. The next time a disaffected minority lost a presidential election, it would invoke the precedent of 1860 and go out of the Union. Monarchists and reactionaries throughout the world would rejoice in the fulfillment of their prediction that this upstart democracy in North America could not last. Lincoln's refusal to accept disunion *or* compromise eventually brought Greeley around to the same position. In the process, though, Lincoln the hedgehog had to bristle his spines against an even wilier fox than Greeley.

William H. Seward had not fully accepted his eclipse as leader of the Republican party by Lincoln's nomination and election as president. Seward not only aspired to be the "premier" of the Lincoln administration; he also emerged as the foremost Republican advocate of conciliation toward the South during the secession winter. Seward's "Higher Law" and "Irrepressible Conflict" speeches had made him the South's *bête noire* during the 1850s. But in January 1861 he wrote to Lincoln that "every thought that we think ought to be conciliatory, forbearing and patient" toward the South.[11] Lincoln was willing to go along partway with this advice. But Seward flirted with the idea of supporting the Crittenden Compromise, whose centerpiece was an extension of the Missouri Compromise line of 36° 30' between slavery and freedom to all present and future territories. This would have been a repudiation of the platform on which the Republicans had stood from the beginning, and on which they had just won the election.

Lincoln could not countenance this. "Entertain no proposition for a compromise in regard to the *extension* of slavery," he wrote to key Republican leaders including Seward. Crittenden's compromise "would lose us everything we gained by the election. . . . Filibustering for all South of us, and making slave states would follow . . . to put us again on the high-road to a slave empire." The proposal for Republican territorial concessions, Lincoln pointed out, "acknowledges that slavery has equal rights with liberty, and surrenders all we have contended for. . . . We have just carried an election on principles fairly stated to the people. Now we are told in advance, the government shall be broken up, unless we surrender to those we have beaten. . . . If we surrender, it is the end of us. They will repeat the experiment upon us *ad libitum*. A year will not pass, till we shall have to take Cuba as a condition upon which they will stay in the Union."[12]

Lincoln's firmness stiffened Seward's backbone. But it did not end his desire to dominate the administration. The next contest between this fox and the hedgehog occurred over the issue of Fort Sumter. As Seward's biographer put it, during the Sumter crisis "Seward's mind moved restlessly from one possibility to another."[13] He emerged as leader of a faction that wanted to withdraw Union troops from the fort and yield it to the Confederacy. He hoped that this would reassure southern Unionists of the government's peaceful intent, thereby keeping the upper South in the Union and cooling passions in the lower South.

Most of the cabinet and General-in-Chief Winfield Scott seemed at first to concur with this policy. Only Postmaster-General Montgomery Blair shared Lincoln's conviction that to give up Sumter would constitute a recognition of Confederate legitimacy and thus concede the principles of Unionism and national sovereignty. With the help of Blair's brother-in-law Gustavus Fox, Lincoln devised a plan to re-supply the garrison at Sumter in such a way as to put the onus of starting a war on the Confederacy if southern artillery tried to stop the supply ships.

When Seward learned of this, he panicked. On his own authority he had clandestinely assured Confederate commissioners that Sumter would be evacuated. Now all his foxy maneuvers would be exposed as deceitful if not worse. In apparent desperation he sent to Lincoln his April Fool's Day memorandum. But Seward meant it seriously. It was a perfect illustration of Isaiah Berlin's definition of the fox as one whose thought is "scattered or diffused, moving on many levels." Contending that the administration lacked a "policy" to deal with secession, Seward suggested one and offered to carry it out in his self-assumed role as premier of the administration. He would give up Fort Sumter but reinforce the other principal southern fort in Union possession, Fort Pickens guarding Pensacola harbor. This, said Seward mysteriously, would *"change the question before the Public from one upon Slavery, or about Slavery for a question upon Union and Disunion."* (Seward had convinced himself that only antislavery Republicans wanted to hold Sumter, while all factions in the North wanted to hold the less controversial and more easily reinforced Pickens as a symbol of national sovereignty.) Seward then proposed to provoke a war with Spain or France by demanding explanations from them for their interventionist policies in Santo Domingo and Mexico. This presumably would reunite North and South in a mutual crusade to enforce the Monroe Doctrine.[14]

What Lincoln thought privately of this bizarre memorandum from his secretary of state is unknown. The president's formal reply to Seward was temperate but resolute, as befit a hedgehog. He dismissed the suggestion of a foreign war by ignoring it. As for the critical matter of the forts, Lincoln could "not perceive how the re-inforcement of Fort Sumpter [*sic*] would be done on a slavery, or party issue, while that of Fort Pickens would be on a more national, and patriotic one." He reminded Seward that the government did have a "policy" on the forts, announced a month earlier in Lincoln's inaugural address: "to hold, occupy, and possess the property and places belonging to the government." That was still the policy; Lincoln was determined to carry it out even at the risk of war over Sumter. And "if this must be done," he concluded pointedly, "*I* must do it."[15]

Like Lincoln's courtroom adversary described by Leonard Swett, Seward had landed on his back in a ditch. And he knew it. He no longer had any illusions about who was to be the premier of this administration. Seward became one of Lincoln's most loyal and trusted subordinates. Lincoln repaid that loyalty by protecting Seward against an attempt by Republican senators to force him from the cabinet in December 1862—another notable occasion when the hedgehog outwitted several foxes.

After April 1861, Horace Greeley became one of the most prominent men who played fox to Lincoln's hedgehog. An early wartime instance of this occurred in the days after the Union defeat at Bull Run on July 21, 1861. In the weeks before this battle, the banner headlines "FORWARD TO RICHMOND" in Greeley's *New York Tribune* had contributed to the pressure that prodded the army into what turned out to be a premature offensive. From a feeling of remorse, or panic, Greeley suffered something of a nervous breakdown after the battle. "This is my seventh sleepless night," he began a letter to Lincoln on July 29. "On every brow sits sullen, black despair. . . . If the Union is irrevocably gone, an armistice for thirty, sixty, ninety, one hundred and twenty days—better still for a year—ought at once to be proposed, with a view to a peaceful adjustment. . . . If it is better for the country and for mankind that we make peace with the rebels at once, and on their own terms, do not shrink even from that."[16]

Lincoln too endured some sleepless nights after Bull Run, but he did not deviate a hair's breadth from his central vision of preserving the Union by winning the war. Lincoln's secretary John Nicolay wrote two days after the battle that "the fat is in the fire now. . . . Preparations for the war will be continued with increased vigor by the government." While Greeley was writing in despair to Lincoln, the president was outlining military strategy in a pair of memoranda which called for intensifying the blockade, increasing the army, and pushing forward offensives in Virginia and Tennessee.[17] In essence, this remained Lincoln's determined policy until Appomattox, through victory and defeat and frustration with incompetent or irresolute military commanders. It was a policy sustained by the spirit manifested in a letter Lincoln wrote during the Seven Days battles in 1862, another Union defeat that plunged many northerners into a despondency that matched Greeley's a year earlier. "I expect to maintain this contest," declared Lincoln, "until successful, or till I die, or am conquered, or my term expires, or Congress or the country forsakes me."[18]

By 1864 this meant prosecuting the war until Confederate forces surrendered unconditionally. But by midsummer of that year the prospects of accomplishing this goal seemed bleak. The two principal Union armies had suffered nearly 100,000 casualties without fulfilling the high hopes of spring that Richmond and Atlanta would fall and the war end by the Fourth of July. War weariness and a desire for peace—perhaps even peace at any price—crept over the North. "Who shall revive the withered hopes that bloomed at the opening of Grant's campaign?" asked the *New York World* in July. "Patriotism is played out," declared another Democratic newspaper. "All are tired of this damnable tragedy."[19] In the midst of his campaign for reelection, it appeared that Lincoln would lose to a Democrat running on a peace platform. In August, Lincoln himself fully expected to lose. Other Republicans were equally pessimistic. "Lincoln's reelection is an impossibility" unless he can bring peace or victory, wrote Seward's alter ego Thurlow Weed. "The people are wild for peace."[20]

During this grave crisis—perhaps the gravest of Lincoln's presidency—Horace Greeley set in motion a peace overture that once more contrasted Lincoln's steady focus with Greeley's mercurial wavering. Learning of the presence of Confederate agents at Niagara Falls, Canada, Greeley wrote Lincoln urging him to explore with them the possibility of peace negotiations. "Our bleeding, bankrupt, almost dying country also longs for peace—shudders at the prospect of fresh conscriptions, wholesale devastations, and of new rivers of human blood." Seeing an opportunity to use Greeley to expose the impossibility of securing peace by negotiations except on Confederate terms, Lincoln immediately authorized him to bring to Washington under safe conduct "any person anywhere professing to have any proposition of Jefferson Davis in writing, for peace, embracing the restoration of the Union and the abandonment of slavery."[21]

Of course no such person existed, and Lincoln knew it. There followed a comic-opera scenario in which Greeley tried to wriggle out of responsibility for carrying through the initiative he had set in motion while Lincoln pressed him to go forward. Reluctantly Greeley did so, eliciting just what Lincoln expected and wanted—public statements from Confederate leaders that they would negotiate no peace that did not include independence. An embarrassed Greeley squirmed and twisted, trying to shift the blame to Lincoln in a private letter that condemned the president's strategy of unconditional surrender as a "fatuity." "No truce! No armistice! No negotiation! No mediation! Nothing but surrender at discretion!" Greeley exclaimed. "There is nothing like it in history. It must result in disaster, or all experience is delusive." Never mind that this had been pretty much the policy advocated by the *Tribune* during the three years between Greeley's crises of confidence in July 1861 and July 1864. Greeley now believed that "no Government fighting a rebellion should ever close its ears to any proposition the rebels may make."[22]

But Lincoln had a firmer grip on reality. He pointed out in his annual message to Congress on December 6, 1864, that Jefferson Davis had repeatedly made it clear that his terms for peace were independence and nothing less. "He does not attempt to deceive us," said Lincoln. "He affords us no excuse to deceive ourselves. He cannot voluntarily reaccept the Union; we cannot voluntarily yield it. Between him and us the issue is distinct, simple, and inflexible. It is an issue that can only be tried by war, and decided by victory."[23] When Lincoln said this, of course, military fortunes had turned decisively in favor of Union victory. But that only vindicated the steadfast sagacity of Lincoln's refusal to give in to despair and defeatism during the dark days of the previous summer.

The peace-negotiations exchange between Lincoln and Greeley involved the issue of slavery as well as that of Union. Clever disinformation tactics by Confederate agents and northern Peace Democrats had spread the notion that only Lincoln's insistence on emancipation as a prior condition of negotiations prevented peace. Greeley seems to have bought this line, at least temporarily. "We do not contend," he wrote in the *Tribune* on July 25, "that reunion is possible or endurable only on the basis of Universal Freedom. . . . War has its exigencies which cannot be foreseen . . . and Peace is often desirable on other terms than those of our choice." If this meant anything, it meant that Greeley was willing to drop emancipation as a condition. Though the pressure on Lincoln from even staunch Republicans to do the same became so intense that the president almost caved in, he ultimately stood fast. He denied that he was "now carrying on this war for the sole purpose of abolition. It is & will be carried on so long as I am President for the sole purpose of restoring the Union. But no human power can subdue this rebellion without using the Emancipation lever as I have done." The Emancipation Proclamation was a solemn promise. To break it in a chimerical quest for peace would be "a cruel and astounding breach of faith" for which "I should be damned in time & eternity. . . . The world shall know that I will keep my faith to friends & enemies, come what will."[24]

Greeley and Lincoln appeared to have switched sides since their exchange of public letters on emancipation two years earlier. On that occasion Greeley had castigated the president for his reluctance to adopt emancipation as a war policy. Lincoln had replied with the famous words: "My paramount object in this struggle *is* to save the Union, and is *not* either to save or to destroy slavery. If I could save the Union without freeing any slave I would do it, and if I could save it by freeing *all* the slaves I would do it; and if I could save it by freeing some and leaving others alone I would also do that."[25] In 1864 Lincoln's critics were asking him to revert to the first or third of these alternatives—to free none or only some of the slaves—while he was now committed to the second one of freeing all, since he supported the Thirteenth Amendment, passed by the Senate and endorsed by the Republican platform on which he was running for reelection. There was no inconsistency between the Lincoln of 1862 and the Lincoln of 1864; on both occasions his paramount object was to save the Union, with emancipation as a potential "lever" to help do the job. In 1864 he was convinced that the lever was essential; in August 1862 he had also been convinced of this, though he was then waiting for a propitious time to announce it. It was Greeley, not Lincoln, who zig-zagged on slavery between 1862 and 1864.

Yet there was an apparent contradiction in Lincoln's position on slavery. To resolve that contradiction will go to the heart of the theme of Lincoln as hedgehog. Lincoln had always considered slavery "an unqualified evil to the negro, the white man, and the State."[26] If anything had been the "single central vision" of his political career before 1861, it had been this. A study of Lincoln as a public speaker maintains that the 175 speeches he gave from 1854 to 1860 showed him to be a "one-issue man" whose "central message" was the necessity of excluding slavery from the territories as the first step toward putting the institution on the path to ultimate extinction.[27]

The Declaration of Independence was the foundation of Lincoln's political philosophy. "I have never had a feeling politically that did not spring from the sentiments embodied in the Declaration," he said in 1861. Lincoln insisted that the phrase "all men are created equal" applied to black people as well as to whites. This powered his conviction that the Founders had looked toward the ultimate extinction of slavery. That is why they did not mention the words "slave" or "slavery" in the Constitution. "Thus the thing is hid away, in the constitution," said Lincoln in 1854, "just as an afflicted man hides away a wen or cancer, which he dares not cut out at once, lest he bleed to death; with the promise, nevertheless, that the cutting may begin at the end of a given time."[28]

These were the principles that for Lincoln made America stand for something unique and important in the world; they were the principles that the heroes of the Revolution whom Lincoln revered had fought and died for; without these principles the United States would become just another oppressive autocracy. That is why the Kansas-Nebraska Act propelled Lincoln back into politics in 1854; that is what fueled the 175 speeches he gave during the next six years. The repeal of the Missouri Compromise restriction on slavery's expansion seemed to legitimize the permanence of the institution; Stephen A. Douglas's statement that he cared not whether slavery was voted down or up represented a despicable moral indifference; Douglas's denial that Negroes were included in the phrase "all men are created equal" was a lamentable declension from the faith of the fathers. "Near eighty years ago we began by declaring that all men are created equal," said Lincoln at Peoria in 1854, "but now from that beginning we have run down to the other declaration, that for some men to enslave others is 'a sacred right of self-government.' . . . Our republican robe is soiled, and trailed in the dust. Let us repurify it. . . . Let us re-adopt the Declaration of Independence, and with it, the practices, and policy, which harmonize with it. . . . If we do this, we shall not only have saved the Union; but we shall have saved it, as to make, and keep it, forever worthy of the saving."[29]

In his famous "lost speech" at Bloomington in 1856, Lincoln said, according to the only contemporary summary of the speech, that "the *Union must be preserved in the purity of its principles as well as in the integrity of its territorial parts.* It must be 'Liberty and Union, now and forever, one and inseparable.' " Note that Lincoln here placed liberty first and Union second; the Union was a *means* to promote the greater *end* of liberty; it was the promise of liberty that made the Union meaningful. In his speech at Independence Hall on Washington's Birthday 1861, Lincoln made the same point more dramatically. The principle of universal liberty in the Declaration of Independence, he told a cheering crowd, was what had kept the United States together for eighty-five years. "But, if this country cannot be saved without giving up that principle—I was about to say I would rather be assassinated on this spot than to surrender it."[30]

Yet when Lincoln became president, he assured southerners that he had no intention of interfering with slavery in their states. When war broke out, he reassured loyal slaveholders on this score, and revoked orders by Union generals emancipating the slaves of Confederates in Missouri and in the South Atlantic states. This was a war for Union, not for liberty, said Lincoln over and over again—to Greeley in August 1862, for example: "If I could save the Union without freeing any slave I would do it." In a letter to his old friend Senator Orville Browning of Illinois on September 22, 1861—ironically, exactly one year before issuing the preliminary Emancipation Proclamation—Lincoln rebuked Browning for his support of General John C. Frémont's order purporting to free the slaves of Confederates in Missouri. "You speak of it as being the only means of *saving* the government. On the contrary it is itself the surrender of government." If left standing, it would drive the border slave states into the Confederacy. "These all against us, and the job on our hands is too large for us. We would as well consent to separation at once, including the surrender of this capitol."[31] To keep the border states—as well as northern Democrats—in the coalition fighting to suppress the rebellion, Lincoln continued to resist antislavery pressures for an emancipation policy well into the second year of the war.

The Union—with or without slavery—had became the one big thing, the "single central vision" of Lincoln the hedgehog. What accounted for this apparent reversal of priorities from liberty first to Union first?—from Union as a means to promote liberty to Union as an end in itself? Mainly it was the responsibility of power, and Lincoln's conception of constitutional limitations on that power. As president, Lincoln had taken an oath to preserve, protect, and defend the Constitution. This duty constrained his options. "I am naturally anti-slavery," he said in an 1864 letter explaining these constraints. "If slavery is not wrong, nothing is wrong. . . . Yet I have never understood that the Presidency conferred upon me an unrestricted right to act officially on this judgment and feeling." His oath of office "forbade me to practically indulge my primary abstract judgment on the moral question of slavery." The Constitution protected slavery; Lincoln was sworn to protect the Constitution.[32]

But wars generate a radical momentum of their own. As Lincoln expressed it in the same letter: "I claim not to have controlled events, but confess plainly that events have controlled me." By 1862 the limited conflict to suppress an insurrection had become a total war in which both sides were trying to mobilize all of their resources. It was becoming clear that the necessity of deferring to border-state and Democratic opinion on slavery was outweighed by the necessity to strike at one of the Confederacy's principal resources—its labor force—and to avoid alienating antislavery northerners, who provided the driving energy and commitment crucial to winning the war. Lincoln's conception of the constitutional relationship between slavery and Union shifted during 1862. "My oath to preserve the constitution," he explained two years later, "imposed upon me the duty of preserving, by every indispensable means, that government—that nation—of which that constitution was the organic law." Lincoln decided in the summer of 1862 to use his war powers as commander in chief to seize enemy property employed to wage war against the United States; he proclaimed the emancipation of the principal form of that property as a "military necessity" to help win the war.

Lincoln used one of his favorite metaphors to illustrate the point. "By general law life *and* limb must be protected; yet often a limb must be amputated to save a life. . . . I felt that measures, otherwise unconstitutional, might become lawful, by becoming indispensable to the preservation of the constitution, through preservation of the nation." When he revoked Frémont's emancipation order in September 1861, he did not think the indispensable necessity to amputate that diseased limb of slavery had come. Nor had it come by May 1862, when Lincoln revoked a similar order by General David Hunter for the South Atlantic states. But in the dark days of defeat during the summer of 1862, the time came. "Driven to the alternative of either surrendering the Union, and with it, the Constitution, or of laying strong hand on the colored element[,] I chose the latter."[33]

The Emancipation Proclamation and its corollary, the enlistment of black troops, did help to win the war and preserve the nation. They were also, of course, crucial steps in the abolition of slavery. All of this is well known. Less often noted is another important fact about the Emancipation Proclamation: it also liberated Abraham Lincoln from the agonizing contradiction between his "oft-expressed *personal* wish that all men everywhere could be free" and his oath of office as president of a slaveholding republic.[34] It fused the "organizing principle" of liberty that guided Lincoln before 1861 with the "single central vision" of Union that became his lodestar during the war. Liberty and Union became "the one big thing" instead of two big things, enabling Lincoln to become a true hedgehog. The "new birth of freedom" that he invoked at Gettysburg restored the Union to the role envisaged for it by the Founders: a means to achieve the end of liberty. And in hedgehog fashion, Lincoln expressed in his second inaugural address a steadfast determination to stick with his policy of total war to total victory even "if God wills that it continue, until all the wealth piled by the bond-man's two hundred and fifty years of unrequited toil shall be sunk, and until every drop of blood drawn with the lash, shall be paid by another drawn with the sword."[35]

VII Liberty and Power in the Second American Revolution

In January 1867, Congressman George W. Julian of Indiana, one of the most radical of Republicans, stood up in the House to speak against a Reconstruction bill that would replace military rule with civil government in the South. Although the measure disfranchised many ex-Confederates and enfranchised former slaves, Julian warned that restoration of these states to self-government "would be ruinous to the best interests of their loyal people and calamitous to the nation." To withdraw the army would "fatally hedge up the way of justice and equality. . . . What these regions need, above all things, is not an easy and quick return to their forfeited rights in the Union, but government, the strong arm of power, outstretched from the central authority here in Washington, making it safe for the freedmen of the South."[1]

Julian's words seemed to express a startling reversal of traditional political philosophy. For a century or more, Americans had regarded centralized power as the greatest threat to liberty. From the Stamp Act crisis to the Jacksonian crusade against the Monster Bank, eternal vigilance against the expansion of power had been the price of liberty. "There is a tendency in all Governments to an augmentation of power at the expense of liberty," wrote James Madison in words echoed by countless Whigs of the Revolutionary generation. To curb this tendency, framers of the Constitution devised a series of checks and balances that divided power among three branches of the national government, between two houses of Congress, and among the state and federal governments as an "essential precaution in favor of liberty." Alexander Hamilton tried to reassure Americans, in *Federalist* No. 28, that state governments would provide them with "security against invasions of the public liberty by national authority."[2]

But this fragmentation and dilution of authority was not enough for libertarians who wished to "restrain . . . power from swelling into tyranny and oppression." They insisted on a bill of rights which, in the first ten amendments to the Constitution, imposed a straitjacket of thou shalt nots on the federal government. When that government nevertheless, in the Sedition Act of 1798, seemed to violate the First Amendment, Thomas Jefferson wrote the Kentucky Resolutions which asserted the right of each state to "judge for itself" the legitimacy of federal laws and "to nullify of their own authority all assumptions of power" they considered unconstitutional. A generation later Jefferson's political heirs scotched the Second Bank of the United States because they believed such a combination of private wealth and government power would, in Andrew Jackson's words, cause "our liberties to be crushed."[3]

No threat of augmented government power was too small to escape the vigilance of Jacksonian Democrats. In 1854, President Franklin Pierce vetoed a bill granting public lands to the states to subsidize mental hospitals. He did so to preserve liberty. For if Congress could do this, warned Pierce, "it has the same power to provide for the indigent who are not insane, and thus . . . the whole field of public beneficence is thrown open to the care and culture of the Federal Government." This would mean "all sovereignty vested in an absolute consolidated central power, against which the spirit of liberty has so often and in so many countries struggled in vain." The bill for mental hospitals, therefore, would be "the beginning of the end . . . of our blessed inheritance of representative liberty."[4]

On the eve of the Civil War most Americans agreed with John Stuart Mill's definition of liberty as "protection against the tyranny of the political rulers." The United States government, observed Thomas Carlyle, consisted of "anarchy, plus a street constable."[5] How, then, could George Julian (whose libertarian credentials were second to none) take a position so strikingly at odds with this legacy? How could he advocate the occupation of states by a standing army, that gravest of threats to republican liberty?

The answer lies in the experience of the second American Revolution—the Civil War of 1861–65 and the painful years of Reconstruction that followed. This experience transformed the relationship between liberty and power—at least for a time. The crux of the transformation was slavery, an institution embedded in the framework of American liberty from the beginning. Samuel Johnson had noted this paradox in the North American colonies in 1775. "How is it," he asked, "that we hear the loudest yelps for liberty among the drivers of negroes?"[6] Thomas Jefferson envisioned the Louisiana Purchase and subsequent territorial acquisitions as an "Empire of Liberty" to ensure the survival of republican freedoms by perpetuation of the land-owning yeomanry whose sturdy independence was the bedrock of American liberty. From 1812 through 1845, however, all five of the states carved out of these territorial acquisitions were slave states. That did not bother most southern whites. By the 1840s they considered slavery a positive good and defended their right of property in slaves as one of the most sacred of republican liberties. This conviction fueled their attempts in 1850 to open the territory conquered from Mexico to slavery and in 1854 to reopen all of the Louisiana Purchase to slavery by repealing the Missouri Compromise provision that had banned the institution north of 36° 30′.

These efforts to promote southern liberty by the expansion of slavery provoked northern antislavery forces to create the powerful new political coalition they named the Republican party. The man whom this party elected as its first president in 1860 had often expressed his view of the relationship between chattel slavery and republican liberty. Perhaps with an eye toward Samuel Johnson's question, Abraham Lincoln said that "the monstrous injustice of slavery . . . deprives our republican example of its just influence in the world—enables the enemies of free institutions, with plausibility, to taunt us as hypocrites." Lincoln believed that the charter of American liberty meant just what it said—*all* men, black as well as white, were created with an equal and inalienable right to liberty. "Near eighty years ago we began by declaring that all men are created equal," said Lincoln, "but now from that beginning we have run down to that other declaration, that for some men to enslave others is a 'sacred right of self-government.' . . . That perfect liberty they sigh for [is] the liberty of making slaves of other people." "These principles cannot stand together," insisted Lincoln. "Our republican robe is soiled, and trailed in the dust. Let us repurify it." The way to do so, said Lincoln in his House Divided address of 1858, was to restrict the further expansion of slavery as the first step to putting it on the road to "ultimate extinction."[7]

Southerners took Lincoln at his word. When he won the presidency they left the Union to escape the "ultimate extinction" of slavery. They did so in the name of the republican liberty for which their forebears had fought. The "liberty loving people" of Alabama acted in "the same spirit of freedom and independence that impelled our Fathers to the separation from the British Government," declared secessionists in that state. Confederate volunteers rushed to enlist in "this second revolution . . . for liberty & human rights."[8] But for Lincoln and most northerners, the South's profession to fight for liberty was a mockery—"the liberty of making slaves of other people." A successful rebellion by the Confederacy would mean the destruction of the United States—destruction of that "new nation, conceived in liberty" brought forth by the founding fathers in 1776 as "the last best, hope" for the survival of republican liberties in the world. "Our popular government has often been called an experiment," Lincoln told Congress on July 4, 1861. "Two points in it, our people have already settled—the successful *establishing,* and the successful *administering* of it. One still remains—its successful maintenance against a formidable internal attempt to overthrow it."[9]

No word except "treason" was more common in the North to describe secession than "anarchy"; Lincoln called it "the essence of anarchy."[10] This reflected a prominent theme in libertarian thought. The twin dangers to liberty were tyranny on one extreme and anarchy, or "licentiousness," on the other. License was the abuse of liberty, the aggressive exercise of liberty without restraints imposed by regard for the rights and liberties of others. It was Thomas Hobbes's state of nature, a war of each against all in which unrestrained liberty exercised by the strong destroyed or enslaved the weak. To prevent this and to provide ordered liberty restrained by wholesome laws, men entered into the social contract called government—"to secure the Blessings of Liberty," as the preamble of the Constitution phrased it. "Liberty does not consist in living without restraint," insisted Whigs of the Revolutionary generation. "Nothing next to *slavery* is more to be dreaded, than the anarchy and confusion that will ensue, if proper regard is not paid to the good and wholesome laws of government."[11]

The American Civil War, according to Lincoln, was a contest to defend ordered liberty against a lawless effort by rebels to "break up their Government, and thus practically put an end to free government upon the earth. It forces us to ask: 'Is there, in all republics, this inherent, and fatal weakness?' 'Must a government, of necessity, be too *strong* for the liberties of its own people, or too *weak* to maintain its own existence?' " Lincoln answered his rhetorical question in the negative. "No choice was left but to call out the war power of the Government; and so to resist force, employed for its destruction, by force, for its preservation."[12] Unprecedented power had become necessary to defend liberty against unprecedented peril.

By the time of Lincoln's Gettysburg Address in 1863, the Union government was using this power in behalf of "a new birth of freedom" for the nation—and for its four million slaves. Above all else, this was what made the Civil War, in the words of Karl Marx, a "world-transforming . . . revolutionary movement."[13] At the core of this second American Revolution was a fundamental transformation in the relationship between power and liberty. Southern slaveholders had exercised their asserted liberty of self-government to protect their "liberty of making slaves of other people," as Lincoln had once put it sarcastically. In April 1864 he noted that "the processes by which thousands are daily passing from under the yoke of bondage [is] hailed by some as the advance of liberty, and bewailed by others as the destruction of all liberty."[14]

Lincoln left no doubt of his convictions concerning the correct definition of liberty. And as commander in chief of an army of one million men armed with the most advanced weapons in the world, he wielded a great deal of power. In April 1864 this army was about to launch offensives that would produce casualties and destruction unprecedented even in this war that brought death to more Americans than all the country's other wars combined. Yet this was done in the name of liberty—to preserve the republic "conceived in liberty" and to bring a "new birth of freedom" to the slaves. As Lincoln conceived it, power was the protector of liberty, not its enemy—except to the liberty of those who wished to do as they pleased with the product of other men's labor.

Isaiah Berlin's distinction between negative and positive liberty is useful to explain the transformation wrought by the Civil War in the relationship between power and liberty. Negative liberty is freedom *from* interference by outside authority with individual thought or behavior. Positive liberty is freedom *to* achieve a status of freedom previously denied by disability or law.[15] Negative liberty is vulnerable to power; positive liberty is a form of power. Defense of negative liberty from an excess of power was a dominant concern of Americans—especially Jeffersonians, Jacksonians, and southerners—from the Revolution to the Civil War. The Bill of Rights is a classic expression of negative liberty. Slaveholders relied on this same conception of negative liberty to guard their right of property in human beings from interference by the national government. John C. Calhoun and other southern political philosophers constructed an elaborate structure of state sovereignty and limitations on national power to buttress their "liberty of making slaves of other people." No exercise of government power—not even support for mental hospitals—escaped the attention of these proslavery libertarians. "If Congress can make banks, roads, and canals under the Constitution," declared Nathaniel Macon of North Carolina, "they can free any slave in the United States."[16]

When southern libertarians invoked state sovereignty to break up the Union, this extreme of negative liberty became "the essence of anarchy" in the eyes of most Americans. Secession and slavery became identified with treason; the military power of the national government became identified with Union and freedom. This helped change the course of American constitutional development. Eleven of the first twelve amendments to the Constitution limited the powers of the national government; six of the next seven dramatically expanded those powers at the expense of states and individuals. In place of the "shall nots" of ten of the first eleven amendments, the six postwar amendments included the phrase "Congress *shall have the power* to enforce this article" (italics added).

Positive liberty achieved by overwhelming power was the fruition of the second American Revolution. The Republican majority in Congress believed that this liberty could not be sustained without the continued and even expanded application of national authority. "The power of the great landed aristocracy in [the South], if unrestrained by power from without, would inevitably [re]assert itself," said George Julian in his 1867 speech quoted at the beginning of this essay. And Congressman James Garfield added that "we must lay the heavy hand of military authority upon these rebel communities, and . . . plant liberty on the ruins of slavery."[17] How to accomplish this would become the central problem of Reconstruction.

The American vision of republican liberty encompassed more than simple freedom; it included also the civil and political equality of freemen. Governments derive "their just power from the consent of the governed," wrote Jefferson in the Declaration of Independence. Those "who have *no* Voice nor Vote in the Electing of *Representatives, do not enjoy* Liberty," declared other spokesmen of the Revolutionary generation. "To be enslaved, is to have Governors whom *other Men have set over us,* and to be subject to laws *made by the Representatives of Others.*"[18]

Black leaders and their white allies made this principle the cornerstone of their definition of liberty during the second American Revolution. In October 1864 a National Convention of Colored Citizens met at Syracuse, New York, and issued an "Address to the People of the United States" written by Frederick Douglass. "In a republican country," said Douglass, "where general suffrage is the rule, personal liberty . . . and all other rights, become mere privileges held at the option of others, where we are excepted from the political liberty. . . . The possession of that right [of suffrage] is the keystone to the arch of human liberty." In New Orleans the French-speaking *gens de couleur* proclaimed with passion that there could be no *liberté* without *égalité*. "Emancipation is one fact, and effective liberty is another," their newspaper declared. "No Pariahs in America! . . . Liberty must be the same for all men. If liberty is qualified, those who possess the least rights are not really free. We demand, therefore . . . the right to vote and the right to be judged, treated, and governed according to equal laws."[19]

White abolitionists and radical Republicans took the same position. Without the right to vote, said Wendell Phillips in 1865, "freedom, so called, is a sham. . . . I do not believe in an English freedom that trusts the welfare of the dependent class to the good will and moral sense of the upper class. . . . Our philosophy of government, since the 4th day of July, 1776, is that no class is safe, no freedom is real . . . which does not place in the hands of the man himself the power to protect his own rights." Thaddeus Stevens asked rhetorically how the United States could be a "true Republic" when "twenty-five million of a privileged class exclude five million from all participation in the rights of government. . . . Without such consent government is a tyranny, and you exercising it are tyrants." Even moderate Republicans came to this position soon after the war and were willing to use the new-fashioned revolutionary power of the national government to mandate black suffrage. While conceding that "to introduce to the voting franchise four millions of [freed] slaves is a revolution," the lawyer Richard

Henry Dana (author of *Two Years before the Mast*) insisted in 1865 that "if we do not secure that now in the time of revolution, it can never be secured except by a new revolution."[20]

How could the freed slaves acquire this instrument of liberty in a federal system where voter qualifications had always been defined by the states? Dana maintained that the national government should act while its armies still held the South in "the grasp of war." But this would not provide a constitutional basis for continuing enforcement of the right. So Republicans rediscovered the guarantee clause of the Constitution. Article IV, Section 4 states that "the United States shall guarantee to every State in this Union a Republican Form of Government." The same article requires the national government also to protect states against invasion and domestic violence. In 1787 the constitutional convention met in the shadow of Shays's Rebellion and of vague rumors about monarchist plots; this article was an attempt to steer the country between the Scylla of anarchy and the Charybdis of monarchy. The domestic violence and invasion clauses had an active life (in the Whiskey Rebellion and the War of 1812), but the "Republican Form of Government" clause slumbered undisturbed for decades. The Supreme Court ducked an opportunity growing out of Rhode Island's Dorr Rebellion in the 1840s to define "republican form." Some abolitionists invoked the clause to argue that slavery was unconstitutional because unrepublican. But as late as 1860 the guarantee clause remained, in Charles Sumner's words, the "sleeping giant" of the Constitution.[21]

Republicans woke the giant to enforce their notion of liberty in the postwar South. The guarantee clause was "the rampart of human liberty," said Senator Richard Yates of Illinois. It "vests in the Congress of the United States a plenary, supreme, unlimited political jurisdiction," added Representative Henry Winter Davis of Maryland. "So ample is this power," maintained Congressman William Lawrence of Ohio, "that Congress might frame a constitution and say to Virginia, 'That is your constitution; you shall be and are restored under that.' "[22] And how did Congress define a republican form of government? For Charles Sumner "equality before the law, and the consent of the governed are essential elements of a republican government." Sumner's colleague in the House, George Boutwell, declared in 1866 that every state government in the South, where one-third of the male citizens were disfranchised because of race, was "an aristocracy; it is an oligarchy; it is not republican."[23] The Republican majority in Congress agreed. In the Civil Rights Act of 1866, the Reconstruction Acts of 1867, and the Fourteenth and Fifteenth Amendments (ratified in 1868 and 1870) they enacted Sumner's equality before the law and consent of the governed (the male half of them, that is) in all states.

After the enactment of these measures the guarantee clause gradually fell into disuse as Congress and the courts looked mainly to the Fourteenth and Fifteenth Amendments as authority for continued intervention in state affairs. These amendments accomplished what historian Robert J. Kaczorowski has described as nothing less than a "revolution" in American constitutionalism. They transferred the primary definition and enforcement of citizenship rights from the states to the national government. This "revolutionary legal theory . . . so centralized power in the national government that the states as separate and autonomous political entities could have been destroyed."[24] They were not, of course, but for a few years before 1873 the federal courts backed by the United States Army became the principal agencies to enforce liberty and equal rights in the South.

Southern whites and northern Democrats invoked traditional libertarian fears of power to denounce the Fourteenth Amendment. This "dangerous innovation . . . authorizes the Federal Government to come in, as an intermeddler, between a State, and the citizens of a State, in almost all conceivable cases," stated a North Carolina legislative committee. "No enlightened patriot" can fail to view "with profoundest alarm" this "tendency to centralization and consolidation" that had swollen the federal government "into a mighty giant, threatening to swallow up the States. . . . In the interest of liberty . . . this centralizing tendency . . . needs to be checked." A Democratic congressman from New Jersey, with the appropriate name of Andrew Jackson Rogers, echoed these sentiments with a warning that the Fourteenth Amendment portended "a revolution . . . [more] dangerous to liberty" than anything Americans had ever experienced, because it would "take away the power of the States . . . and centralize a consolidated power . . . into one imperial despotism."[25]

Rubbish! replied Republican leaders. "I had in the simplicity of my heart supposed that 'State rights,' being the issue of the war, had been decided," said a senator, while an editor declared that "this deplorable nonsense cost us the war, and the nation's life within an inch." We cannot "slink any longer behind the sham, the miserable evasion, that the protection of personal rights and liberty for every citizen of the United States within the limits of any State belongs entirely to the State."[26] Republican congressmen were quite aware of what they were doing, and why. "I admit that this species of legislation is absolutely revolutionary," said Senator Lot M. Morrill of Maine in a speech on the Civil Rights bill of 1866. "But are we not in the midst of a revolution? . . . No nation hitherto has cherished a liberty so universal. The ancient republics were all exceptional in their liberty; they all had excepted classes, subjected classes. . . . [This] civil and political revolution has changed the fundamental principles of our Government."[27]

In the debates on the Fourteenth Amendment, several Republicans insisted that "for the security and future growth of liberty" it would be "better to invade the judicial power of the State than permit it to invade, strike down, and destroy the civil rights of citizens. . . . We must see to it, that hereafter, personal liberty and personal rights are placed in the keeping of the nation . . . against State authority and State interpretations. . . . The great object of this amendment is, therefore, to restrain the power of the States and compel them at all times to respect these great fundamental guaranties."[28]

For several years federal judges upheld the primacy of national citizenship under the Civil Rights Act of 1866 and the Fourteenth Amendment. They sanctioned the prosecution of violators of freedmen's rights in federal courts. The Thirteenth Amendment, declared Supreme Court Justice Noah Swayne sitting as a circuit court justice in Kentucky in 1867, "reversed and annulled the original policy of the constitution" by making liberty universal and giving the national rather than state governments primary power for its protection. Circuit Court Justice (and future Supreme Court Justice) William B. Woods explained in a ruling of 1871 in Alabama that "by the original constitution citizenship in the United States was a consequence of citizenship in a state. By this clause [of the Fourteenth Amendment] this order of things is reversed."[29]

In 1870–71 this growth of national power to protect liberty reached its apogee with three enforcement acts that expanded the jurisdiction of federal courts over civil and voting rights, and authorized the president to suspend the writ of *habeas corpus* and use the army to break up the Ku Klux Klan. Under these laws the government convicted hundreds of Klansmen. One historian of this effort concluded that "federal judges in the early 1870s were decidedly more successful in enforcing civil rights than the more recent federal judges who were charged with dismantling the Jim Crow system."[30]

The existence of this Jim Crow system still waiting to be dismantled a century after the Civil War has undergirded the "post-revisionist" thesis embraced by many historians in the 1970s that the war and Reconstruction accomplished little or nothing of genuine freedom for slaves. The long, tragic history of sharecropping, peonage, poverty, and lynching would seem to confirm the thesis. In the words of two of these post-revisionist historians, emancipation and Reconstruction brought no "specific changes either in the status of former slaves or in the conditions under which they labored." The Civil War was therefore "a tragedy unjustified by its results." The "new birth of freedom" that Lincoln invoked at Gettysburg "never occurred. Sadly, we must conclude that those dead did die in vain" because "real freedom for the Negro remained much more of a promise, or a hope, than a reality."[31]

Did power do nothing for liberty after all? Was there no second American Revolution for slaves? Recent studies, especially the work of Eric Foner, have swung Reconstruction historiography back toward a more positive, "revisionist" position on these questions. The assurance enjoyed by former slaves that their spouses or children could no longer be sold away from them appears after all to have been a rather "specific change" in their "status." Foner and others also recognize that the vast expansion of political power wielded by the national government *and by the freedmen themselves* for a decade or so after the Civil War made a real difference in the nature of their liberty and even in "the conditions under which they labored." Reconstruction legislatures established public schools for blacks, for the first time, and enacted laws to enhance and protect their economic opportunities and rights. The United States was "unique" among post-emancipation societies, Foner points out, because "the former slaves during Reconstruction enjoyed universal manhood suffrage and a real measure of political power." Channeled through the Republican party with its southern base of black voters, this political power depended on the backing of military force—state militias and the remnants of the Union army that remained in the South—to protect it against counterrevolutionary terror by the Ku Klux Klan and other armed auxiliaries of the Democratic party. So long as this power was employed with determination, as in the militia campaigns (led by former Union army officers) against the Klan in Tennessee and Arkansas, and by the army's suppression of the Klan in 1871–72, black voters exercised their political rights in large numbers. Behind this power of the sword, blacks held a larger proportion of public offices in the South than they do today.[32]

It was the successful southern counterrevolution of the 1870s that wiped out many of the gains of the second American Revolution for the freedmen. A key feature of this counterrevolution was a revival of negative liberty in the form of a weakened national government. Supreme Court decisions offer a stark illustration of this process. The first step backward came, ironically, in a case that had nothing to do with the civil rights of blacks. A group of butchers in New Orleans challenged a state law regulating slaughterhouses that restricted their freedom to practice their trade. The butchers charged that this law abridged their "privileges and immunities" of citizenship as defined by the Fourteenth Amendment. By a 5-4 decision in 1873 the Court ruled against the butchers. The citizenship clause of the Fourteenth Amendment designated all persons born or naturalized in the United States as "citizens of the United States and of the State wherein they reside. No State shall make or enforce any law which shall abridge the privileges or immunities of citizens *of the United States*" (italics added).

Whether or not the omission of an additional phrase "or of the State wherein they reside" was intentional, Justice Samuel Miller, speaking for the majority, seized upon it as justification for overturning the primacy of national citizenship by drawing a distinction between state and national citizenship.

Upon such hairsplitting do great issues sometimes turn. Did the framers of the Fourteenth Amendment intend "to transfer the security and protection of all the civil rights" of citizens "from the State to the Federal Government?" asked Miller. Despite evidence that at least some framers had intended precisely that, and that federal courts had so interpreted the Amendment, Miller answered his rhetorical question with a resounding NO! "So great a departure from the structure and spirit of our institutions" would "fetter and degrade the state governments by subjecting them to the control of Congress." It would "constitute this court a perpetual censor upon all legislation of all the States." No such "radical changes" in "the relations of the State and Federal Governments" could have been intended. Miller then proceeded to define national citizenship so narrowly that nearly all civil rights and liberties important to the freedmen were left to primary state jurisdiction.[33]

The four dissenters in *Slaughterhouse Cases* reasserted the primacy of national citizenship as the principal achievement of the second American Revolution. The Fourteenth Amendment, said Justice Stephen J. Field, was "intended to give practical effect to the Declaration of 1776 of inalienable rights" which "do not derive their existence from [state] legislation, and cannot be destroyed by its power" but are placed "under the guardianship of the national authority."[34] Several framers of the Fourteenth Amendment who were still in Congress also denounced the majority opinion as a "great mistake." The Amendment, one of them insisted, accomplished "a revolution in our form of government in giving Congress a control of matters which had hitherto been confined exclusively to state control."[35]

Although a 5-4 ruling in a case that ostensibly had nothing to do with Reconstruction seemed a narrow mandate for change, it proved to be the first step in a constitutional counterrevolution that restored state rights and negative liberty. In the South this counterrevolution soon gave former slaveowners the power to define the scope of their former slaves' liberty. One consequence of *Slaughterhouse* was a decision by the attorney general to suspend prosecutions of Klansmen under the enforcement acts of 1870 and 1871 until the Supreme Court further clarified the Justice Department's powers in this area.

That clarification was not long in coming. In 1876 the Court handed down its ruling in *U.S. v. Cruikshank*. Originating in Louisiana, this case stemmed from the most outrageous carnage of Reconstruction, the "Colfax massacre" of 1873. About a hundred blacks and three whites had been killed in a shootout that was, in fact, a deliberate massacre. The Justice Department indicted nearly a hundred whites for conspiracy to deprive the black victims of their civil rights. The Supreme Court unanimously dismissed these indictments and declared the relevant sections of the Enforcement Act of 1870 unconstitutional on grounds that the Fourteenth Amendment empowered Congress to legislate only against statutory discrimination by state governments, not against discriminatory actions—even murder—by individuals. It was a reaffirmation of the *Slaughterhouse* ruling that primary jurisdiction over most crimes remained with the states. "There can be no constitutional legislation of congress for directly enforcing the privileges and immunities of citizens of the United States by original proceedings in the courts of the United States," pronounced the Court. The Fourteenth Amendment gave Congress no power to enact "laws for the suppression of ordinary crime within the States. . . . That duty was originally assumed by the States; and it still remains there."[36]

In effect, the Court agreed with the argument of one of the defense attorneys (John Campbell of Alabama, a former Supreme Court Justice who had resigned in 1861 to join the Confederate government) that in matters of political and civil rights, "THE AUTHORITY OF A STATE IS COMPLETE, UNQUALIFIED, AND EXCLUSIVE." To convict the perpetrators of the Colfax massacre would lead to the "entire subversion of the institutions of the States and the immediate consolidation of the whole land into a consolidated empire"—and empires, as everyone knew, were the enemies of liberty.[37]

Supreme Court decisions do not take place in a political vacuum. This ruling reflected a growing disillusionment with the disorder and corruption of Reconstruction. Democrats were winning converts to their argument that retention of a standing army in the South subverted liberty—of whites. The economic depression following the Panic of 1873 added to Republican woes. The party's loss of the House (for the first time in sixteen years) in 1874 caused many Republicans to speak of "unloading" the dead weight of "Carpetbag-Negro" governments before they sank the party. "The truth is," confessed a Republican leader in 1875, "our people are tired out with this worn out cry of 'Southern outrages'!!! Hard times & heavy taxes make them wish the 'nigger,' 'everlasting nigger,' were in —— or Africa." When the Republican governor of Mississippi telegraphed for federal troops to protect black voters from white "rifle clubs" during the state election of 1875, the attorney general rejected this request with the words that "the whole public are tired out with these annual autumnal outbreaks in the South, and the great majority are now ready to condemn any interference on the part of the government. . . . Preserve the peace by the forces in your own state, and let the country see that the citizens of Mississippi, who are . . . largely Republican [i.e., the black majority], have the courage to *fight* for their rights."[38] In what white Mississippians frankly called their "Revolution of 1875," they drove blacks from the polls and regained control of the state. The last three Republican state governments in the South likewise collapsed in 1877 when newly elected President Rutherford B. Hayes, no longer willing to sustain "bayonet rule" there, withdrew federal troops and returned the South to "home rule"—that is, rule by white Democrats.

To Democrats everywhere this marked a return to the system of constitutional liberty instituted by the founding fathers. "In the name of justice and humanity," proclaimed Reverdy Johnson of Maryland, probably the country's foremost Democratic lawyer, when he defended Klansmen under federal indictment in South Carolina, "in the name of those rights for which our fathers fought, you cannot subject the white man to the absolute and unconditional domination of an armed force of a colored race." Another Democratic lawyer, commenting in 1878 on the retreat from Reconstruction, concluded that "the minds of patriotic men were filled with alarm at the centralizing tendency of the government. . . . The prospect that the ancient landmarks of the states were to yield before the advancing strides of an imperial despotism" finally brought the American people to their senses.[39]

That Democrats took this position scarcely qualifies as news. What really returned the second American Revolution full circle to the first Revolution's dread of power as the enemy of liberty was the conversion of numerous Republicans to the same viewpoint. No man was more emblematic of this process than Carl Schurz. A republican revolutionary while a student at Bonn University in the heady days of 1848, Schurz like many other Forty-eighters emigrated to the United States to seek the liberty they had failed to establish in Germany. Finding slavery as well as liberty in America, Schurz helped launch the Republican party, rose to major general commanding an army corps during the war, and became one of the leading Republican senators during Reconstruction. Schurz did as much as anyone to mold Reconstruction, which he called in an 1870 speech supporting a bill to enforce the Fifteenth Amendment "a great revolution" to "ensure the fundamental rights and liberties upon which the whole fabric of free government rests." Schurz scorned the Democrats' incessant harping on "what they euphoniously called local self-government and . . . State sovereignty. . . . In the name of liberty [they] asserted the right of one man, under State law, to deprive another man of his freedom." But "the great Constitutional revolution" brought "the vindication of individual rights by the National power. The revolution found the rights of the individual at the mercy of the States . . . and placed them under the shield of National protection." And how did Democrats respond, Schurz asked rhetorically? "As they once asserted that true liberty implied the right of one man to hold another man as his slave, they will tell you now that they are no longer true freemen in their States because . . . they can no longer deprive other men of their rights."[40]

Thus Schurz the advocate of power to protect liberty. But in 1875 he sang the same tune he had ridiculed when Democrats sang it five years earlier. Those five years had produced Schurz's disillusionment with President Ulysses S. Grant and southern Republicans, and his alliance with Democrats as a leader of the Liberal Republican party in the election of 1872. The event that sparked a memorable Schurz speech in 1875 was the arrest by federal troops of several Louisiana legislators on the floor of the legislature. This was but one more incident in the bloody and Byzantine history of Reconstruction in that state. Since 1872 two governments had contended for legitimacy—a Republican one elected by black voters and protected in the capital at New Orleans by the army, and a Democratic one supported by white voters and controlling the countryside with armed guerrillas organized in "White Leagues." Fighting flared all over the state, including New Orleans where a battle between White Leaguers and state militia left thirty dead in September 1874. The eleven hundred federal troops in the state could do little to control the violence because of the rules of engagement that restrained them. The legislative elections of 1874 resulted in the usual disputed returns. By a parliamentary coup, Democrats organized the lower house in January 1875 and swore in their representatives from disputed districts. The Republican governor appealed to the army commander, who marched soldiers into the legislature and arrested several of the Democrats. The Grant administration upheld the army's action.

This affair caused an uproar around the country. Protest meetings adopted angry resolutions. Many Republicans joined the swelling chorus of concern that "bayonet rule" was undermining traditional liberties. Schurz gave voice to this concern in a speech to the Senate on January 11, 1875. "Our system of republican government is in danger," he proclaimed. "Every American who truly loves his liberty will recognize the cause of his own rights and liberties in the cause of Constitutional government in Louisiana." The "insidious advance of irresponsible power" had drawn sustenance from the argument that it was "by Federal bayonets only that the colored man may be safe." Schurz conceded that "brute force" might make "every colored man perfectly safe, not only in the exercise of his franchise but in everything else. . . . You might have made the National Government so strong that, right or wrong, nobody could resist it." That is "an effective method to keep peace and order. . . . It is employed with singular success in Russia." But "what has in the meantime become of the liberties and rights of all of us?" asked this Forty-eighter who had left Germany to escape just such tyranny. "If this can be done in Louisiana . . . how long will it be before it can be done in Massachusetts and in Ohio? How long before the Constitutional rights of all the States and the self-government of all the people may be trampled under foot? . . . How long before a soldier may stalk into the National House of Representatives, and, pointing to the Speaker's mace, say, 'Take away that bauble'?"[41]

A compromise kept the Republican administration in Louisiana afloat for two more years. But like the others it collapsed when the federal bayonets were removed. Schurz had pronounced the epitaph of the second American Revolution. The positive liberty of centralized power gave way to the negative liberty of decentralized federalism. The pendulum did not swing back until another Republican president—who also happened to be a famous general—launched the "second Reconstruction" three-quarters of a century later by sending units of the crack 101st Airborne Division into Little Rock to protect nine black students at Central High School.

Notes

Preface

1. Quoted in Morton Keller, *Affairs of State: Public Life in Late Nineteenth Century America* (Cambridge, Mass., 1977), 2.

2. Richard Taylor to Samuel L. M. Barlow, Dec. 13, 1865, S. L. M. Barlow Papers, Huntington Library.

3. "Getting Right with Lincoln," in David Donald, *Lincoln Reconsidered: Essays on the Civil War Era*, 2nd ed. (Vintage Books ed., New York, 1961), 3–18.

4. Mario M. Cuomo and Harold Holzer, eds., *Lincoln on Democracy* (English language ed., New York, 1990).

I. The Second American Revolution

1. Garfield to Hinsdale, Jan. 22, 1860, Jan. 15, 1861, Hinsdale to Garfield, Jan. 8, 1860, Jan. 13, 1861, in Mary A. Hinsdale, ed., *Garfield-Hinsdale Letters* (Ann Arbor, 1949), 49, 55, 47, 52.

2. Garfield to Lucretia R. Garfield, Oct. 7, 1862, Feb. 22, 1863, in Frederick D. Williams, ed., *The Wild Life of the Army: Civil War Letters of James A. Garfield* (East Lansing, 1964), 160, 238.

3. Burke A. Hinsdale, ed., *The Works of James Abram Garfield*, 2 vols. (Boston, 1882), I: 4, 6–7, 11, 13–14, 17.

4. *Ibid.*, 86–87.

5. *Ibid.*, 249.

6. Phillips in *New York Tribune*, Jan. 23, 1863; *Liberator*, Aug. 8, 1862; and *National Anti-Slavery Standard*, Nov. 17, 1866; Stevens quoted in T. Harry Williams, *Lincoln and the Radicals* (Madison, 1941), 12; Margaret Shortreed, "The Anti-Slavery Radicals, 1840–1868," *Past and Present*, no. 16 (1959): 77; and Fawn M. Brodie, *Thaddeus Stevens: Scourge of the South* (New York, 1959), 231–32;

H. B. Sargent to John Andrew, Jan. 14, 1862, Andrew Papers, Massachusetts Historical Society.

7. Saul K. Padover, ed. and trans., *Karl Marx on America and the Civil War* (New York, 1972), 263, 264, 272, 260, 237; James M. Allen, *Reconstruction: The Battle for Democracy 1865–1876* (New York, 1937), 149.

8. Georges E. B. Clemenceau, *American Reconstruction,* ed. Fernand Balensperger, translated by Margaret MacVeagh (New York, 1926), 294; Eric Foner, "Thaddeus Stevens, Confiscation, and Reconstruction," in Stanley Elkins and Eric McKitrick, eds., *The Hofstadter Aegis: A Memorial* (New York, 1974), 154.

9. *Boston Post,* quoted in *Liberator,* Feb. 6, 1863; *New York Herald,* May 3, 1865.

10. *Memphis Argus,* quoted in Eugene D. Genovese, *Roll, Jordan, Roll: The World the Slaves Made* (New York, 1974), 110; South Carolinian quoted in Kenneth M. Stampp, *The Era of Reconstruction, 1865–1877* (New York, 1965), 170.

11. Charles A. Beard and Mary R. Beard, *The Rise of American Civilization,* 2 vols. (New York 1927), II: 53–54.

12. Herbert Aptheker, *The American Civil War* (New York, 1961); Allen, *Reconstruction: The Battle for Democracy.*

13. Barrington Moore, Jr., *Social Origins of Dictatorship and Democracy: Lord and Peasant in the Making of the Modern World* (Boston, 1966), 152, 112.

14. See especially Thomas C. Cochran, "Did the Civil War Retard Industrialization?" *Mississippi Valley Historical Review* 48 (1961): 197–210; David T. Gilchrist and W. David Lewis, eds., *Economic Change in the Civil War Era* (Greenville, Del., 1965); and Stanley L. Engerman, "The Economic Impact of the Civil War," *Explorations in Entrepreneurial History,* 2nd Series, 3 (1966): 176–99. Ralph Andreano, ed., *The Economic Impact of the American Civil War* (Cambridge, Mass., 1972), contains several articles relevant to this question, and Patrick O'Brien, *The Economic Effects of the American Civil War* (London, 1988), summarizes the literature and arguments on the issue.

15. Data compiled from Donald B. Dodd and Wynelle S. Dodd, *Historical Statistics of the South 1790–1970* (University, Ala., 1973); Lee Soltow, *Men and Wealth in the United States 1850–1870* (New Haven, 1975); Stanley L. Engerman, "Some Economic Factors in Southern Backwardness in the Nineteenth Century," in John F. Kain and John R. Meyers, eds., *Essays in Regional Economics* (Cambridge, Mass., 1971), 291, 300–302; and James L. Sellers, "The Eco-

nomic Incidence of the Civil War in the South," *Mississippi Valley Historical Review* 14 (1927): 179–91. For additional data and speculations, see Claudia D. Goldin and Frank D. Lewis, "The Economic Cost of the American Civil War: Estimates and Implications," *The Journal of Economic History* 35 (1975): 299–326.

16. Leonard P. Curry, *Blueprint for Modern America: Non-Military Legislation of the First Civil War Congress* (Nashville, 1968).

17. C. Vann Woodward, *American Counterpoint: Slavery and Racism in the North-South Dialogue* (Boston, 1971), 140–83; V. Jacque Voegeli, *Free But Not Equal: The Midwest and the Negro during the Civil War* (Chicago, 1967); William Gillette, *Retreat from Reconstruction 1869–1879* (Baton Rouge, 1979).

18. William S. McFeely, *Yankee Stepfather: General O. O. Howard and the Freedmen* (New Haven, 1968); Louis S. Gerteis, *From Contraband to Freedman: Federal Policy Toward Southern Blacks 1861–1865* (Westport, Conn., 1973); C. Peter Ripley, *Slaves and Freedmen to Civil War Louisiana* (Baton Rouge, 1976); Leon F. Litwack, *Been in the Storm So Long: The Aftermath of Slavery* (New York, 1979); Lawrence N. Powell, *New Masters: Northern Planters During the Civil War and Reconstruction* (New Haven, 1980).

19. Jonathan M. Wiener, *Social Origins of the New South: Alabama 1860–1885* (Baton Rouge, 1978); Jay Mandle, *The Roots of Black Poverty: The Southern Plantation Economy after the Civil War* (Durham, 1978); Dwight D. Billings, *Planters and the Making of a "New South": Class, Politics, and Development in North Carolina 1865–1900* (Chapel Hill, 1979).

20. Gerteis, *From Contraband to Freedman*, 3–5.

21. Alfred Meusel, "Revolution and Counter-Revolution," *Encyclopedia of the Social Sciences*, 13 (1934): 367; Willem F. Wertheim, *Evolution and Revolution: The Rising Waves of Emancipation* (London, 1974), 134; Samuel P. Huntington, *Political Order in Changing Societies* (New Haven, 1968), 264; Crane Brinton, *The Anatomy of Revolution* (New York, 1957), 4; E. H. Carr, "The Russian Revolution: Its Place in History," in Lawrence Kaplan and Carol Kaplan, eds., *Revolutions: A Comparative Study* (New York, 1973), 281.

22. Jacques Ellul, *Autopsy of Revolution*, translated by Patricia Wolf (New York, 1971), ix.

23. U.S. Bureau of the Census, *Historical Statistics of the United States, Colonial Times to 1970* (Washington, 1975), 370, 382.

24. Roger L. Ransom and Richard Sutch, *One Kind of Freedom: The Economic Consequences of Emancipation* (Cambridge, 1977),

pages 4–7; Roger L. Ransom and Richard Sutch, "Growth and Welfare in the American South of the Nineteenth Century," *Explorations in Economic History* 16 (1979): 222–27.

25. Ransom and Sutch, *One Kind of Freedom*, 84; U.S. Bureau of the Census, *Negro Population 1790–1915* (Washington, 1918), 609.

26. Eric Foner, *Reconstruction: America's Unfinished Revolution 1863–1877* (New York, 1988), 449; Foner, *Nothing But Freedom: Emancipation and Its Legacy* (Baton Rouge, 1983), 52, 46; planter quoted in *ibid.*, 53.

27. *Ibid.*, 35; see also Foner, *Reconstruction*, 109.

28. Foner, *Reconstruction*, passim; Daniel A. Novak, *The Wheel of Servitude: Black Forced Labor After Slavery* (Lexington, Ky., 1978); Carol K. Rothrock Bleser, *The Promised Land: The History of the South Carolina Land Commission, 1869–1890* (Columbia, 1969); Foner, *Nothing But Freedom*, 103–5.

29. Clemenceau, *American Reconstruction*, 259.

30. Wilson to William Lloyd Garrison, Dec. 17, 1874, William Lloyd Garrison Papers, Boston Public Library.

II. Lincoln and the Second American Revolution

1. James G. Randall, *Lincoln the Liberal Statesman* (New York, 1947), 178, 177; Roy C. Basler, ed., *The Collected Works of Abraham Lincoln,* 9 vols. (New Brunswick, N.J., 1953–55), II, 272, 273.

2. T. Harry Williams, "Lincoln and the Radicals," in Grady McWhiney, ed., *Grant, Lee, Lincoln and the Radicals: Essays on Civil War Leadership* (Evanston, 1964), 114; Norman A. Graebner, "Abraham Lincoln: Conservative Statesman," in Graebner, ed., *The Enduring Lincoln* (Urbana, 1959), 68.

3. Mark Twain and Charles Dudley Warner, *The Gilded Age* (New American Library ed., New York, 1969), 137–38; Disraeli quoted in Belle Becker Sideman and Lillian Friedman, eds., *Europe Looks at the Civil War* (New York, 1960), 233.

4. *Springfield Republican*, Sept. 24, 1862; Otto Olsen, "Abraham Lincoln as Revolutionary," *Civil War History* 24 (1978): 213–24.

5. *Collected Works of Lincoln*, I, 278, 438; II, 115, 130; Saul K. Padover, ed. and translator, *Karl Marx on America and the Civil War* (New York, 1972), 237.

6. All three quotations are from James Oakes, *The Ruling Race: A History of American Slaveholders* (New York, 1982), 239–40.

7. *Ibid.*, 239; Dunbar Rowland, ed., *Jefferson Davis, Constitu-*

tionalist: His Letters, Papers, and Speeches, 10 vols. (Jackson, 1923), V, 43, 202.

8. George Ward Nichols, The Story of the Great March (New York, 1865), 302; songs quoted in Drew Gilpin Faust, The Creation of Confederate Nationalism: Ideology and Identity in the Civil War South (Baton Rouge, 1988), 14, 91.

9. Frank Moore, ed., The Rebellion Record, VI (New York, 1863), "Documents," 299; William L. Barney, The Secessionist Impulse: Alabama and Mississippi in 1860 (Princeton, 1974), 192; Atlanta Daily Intelligencer, Dec. 13, 1860.

10. New York Evening Post, Feb. 18, 1861; New York Tribune, March 27, 1861, May 21, 1862.

11. De Bow's Review, 33 (1862), 44; Rowland, ed., Jefferson Davis, Constitutionalist, VI, 50, 72, VI, 357.

12. Susan Sparks Keitt to Mrs. Frederick Brown, March 4, 1861, quoted in Steven Channing, Crisis of Fear: Secession in South Carolina (New York, 1970), 287; Columbia Daily South Carolinian, Aug. 3, 1860, in Dwight L. Dumond, Southern Editorials on Secession (New York, 1931), 154.

13. Macon Telegraph, Nov. 8, 1860, quoted in Michael P. Johnson, Toward a Patriarchal Republic: The Secession of Georgia (Baton Rouge, 1977), 46; Official Records of the Union and Confederate Navies in the War of the Rebellion, 30 vols. (Washington, 1894–1922), Ser. II, Vol. 3, pp. 257–58.

14. Collected Works of Lincoln, VIII, 333; IV, 434n.

15. Ibid., IV, 439, 438; V, 53.

16. Moncure Conway, The Rejected Stone: or Insurrection vs. Resurrection in America (Boston, 1861), 75–80, 110; Principia, May 4, 1861; Margaret Shortreed, "The Anti-Slavery Radicals: From Crusade to Revolution 1840–1868," Past and Present, no. 16 (Nov. 1959), 77; Congressional Globe, 37th Cong., 1st sess., p. 414.

17. Collected Works of Lincoln, V, 49; VII, 281.

18. Ibid., V, 144–46, 222–23, 317–19; New York Tribune, July 19, 1862; Gideon Welles, "The History of Emancipation," Galaxy 14 (1872): 842–43.

19. Indiana colonel quoted in Allan Nevins, The War for the Union: War Becomes Revolution (New York, 1960), 230; War of the Rebellion: Official Records of the Union and Confederate Armies, Ser. I, Vol. 24, pt. 3, p. 157; General Grenville Dodge quoted in Bruce Catton, Grant Moves South (Boston, 1960), 294.

20. Collected Works of Lincoln, VI, 149–50, 408–9.

21. *Ibid.,* V, 346, 350; Welles, "History of Emancipation," 842–43.

22. *Collected Works of Lincoln,* VIII, 333.

23. John Bennett Walters, "General William T. Sherman and Total War," *Journal of Southern History* 14 (1948): 463, 470.

24. *Collected Works of Lincoln,* VIII, 73–74, 182.

25. Leonard P. Curry, *Blueprint for Modern America: Nonmilitary Legislation of the First Civil War Congress* (Nashville, 1968); Barrington Moore, Jr., *Social Origins of Dictatorship and Democracy: Lord and Peasant in the Making of the Modern World* (Boston, 1966), 111–65; Gabor S. Boritt, *Lincoln and the Economics of the American Dream* (Memphis, 1978).

26. *Collected Works of Lincoln,* V, 388.

27. *Ibid.,* VIII, 332–33; VII, 282.

III. Lincoln and Liberty

1. Roy P. Basler, ed., *The Collected Works of Abraham Lincoln,* 9 vols. (New Brunswick, N.J., 1953–55), VII, 301–2.

2. John Stuart Mill, *On Liberty* (Harvard Classics ed.), 203; Francis Lieber, *On Civil Liberty and Self-Government* (Philadelphia, 1859), 37; Don E. Fehrenbacher, "Introduction" to David M. Potter, *Freedom and Its Limitations in American Life* (Stanford, 1976), x.

3. Lieber, *On Civil Liberty,* 103; both Adamses quoted in Francis William Coker, ed., *Democracy, Liberty, and Property: Readings in the American Political Tradition* (New York, 1942), 125, 320.

4. The question of Negro citizenship occupies pp. 403–27 of Taney's opinion in *Dred Scott v. Sandford,* 19 Howard 393.

5. *Letters and Speeches of the Hon. James H. Hammond, of South Carolina* (New York, 1866), 317–19.

6. Richard K. Cralle, ed., *The Works of John C. Calhoun,* 6 vols. (New York, 1854–57), IV, 505–6; Yancey quoted in George M. Fredrickson, *The Black Image in the White Mind* (New York, 1971), 61.

7. Quoted in J. Mills Thornton III, *Politics and Power in a Slave Society: Alabama, 1800–1860* (Baton Rouge, 1978), 321; and James Oakes, *The Ruling Race: A History of American Slaveholders* (New York, 1982), 141.

8. *Collected Works of Lincoln,* I, 108, 278; II, 126; IV, 198.

9. *Ibid.,* II, 255, 130; III, 327, 16.

10. *Ibid.,* III, 177, 113.

11. *Ibid.,* II, 323.

12. *Ibid.,* III, 95, 376, 375; II, 250.

13. *Ibid.,* III, 315, 29; II, 276.

14. Alabama newspaper quoted in J. Mills Thornton III, *Politics and Power in a Slave Society: Alabama 1800–1860* (Baton Rouge, 1978), 216; Georgia secessionist quoted in Michael P. Johnson, *Toward a Patriarchal Republic: The Secession of Georgia* (Baton Rouge, 1977), 36.

15. Henry Orr to Mary Orr, Oct. 31, 1861, in John W. Anderson, ed., *Campaigning with Parsons' Texas Cavalry Brigade, CSA* (Hillsboro, Tex., 1967), 10; *LINCOLN ELECTED!* Broadside from Bell County, Texas, Nov. 8, 1860, McLelland Lincoln Collection, John Hay Library, Brown University.

16. Dunbar Rowland, ed., *Jefferson Davis, Constitutionalist: His Letters, Papers, and Speeches,* 10 vols. (Jackson, Miss., 1923), V, 43, 202.

17. *National Anti-Slavery Standard,* Dec. 1, 1860.

18. Tyler Dennett, ed., *Lincoln and the Civil War in the Diaries and Letters of John Hay* (New York, 1939), 19; *Collected Works of Lincoln,* V, 53; IV, 426; VII, 23.

19. *Collected Works of Lincoln,* V, 436–37.

20. Frank Freidel, ed., *Union Pamphlets of the Civil War* (Cambridge, Mass., 1967), 740–43.

21. Quoted in Don E. Fehrenbacher, "The Paradoxes of Freedom," in Fehrenbacher, *Lincoln in Text and Context: Collected Essays* (Stanford, 1987), 135.

22. *Collected Works of Lincoln,* IV, 430; VI, 267.

23. *Ibid.,* VI, 262, 266–67.

24. In Isaiah Berlin, *Four Essays on Liberty* (New York, 1970), 118–72.

25. For a fuller development of this theme, see the final essay in this book, "Liberty and Power in the Second American Revolution."

26. *Collected Works of Lincoln,* IV, 438; V, 537.

IV. Lincoln and the Strategy of Unconditional Surrender

1. Roy P. Basler, ed., *The Collected Works of Abraham Lincoln,* 9 vols. (New Brunswick, N.J., 1953–55), VIII, 333.

2. Earl Schenck Miers, ed., *Lincoln Day by Day: A Chronology 1809–1865,* 3 vols. (Washington, 1960), Vol. III: 1861–1865, ed. by C. Percy Powell.

3. David Homer Bates, *Lincoln in the Telegraph Office* (New York, 1907).

4. Tyler Dennett, ed., *Lincoln and the Civil War in the Diaries and Letters of John Hay* (New York, 1939), 180; *Collected Works of Lincoln,* VII, 393.

5. John Henry Cramer, *Lincoln under Enemy Fire* (New York, 1948).

6. *Collected Works of Lincoln,* VII, 476.

7. Mark E. Neely, Jr., *The Abraham Lincoln Encylopedia* (New York, 1982); Gabor S. Boritt, ed., *The Historian's Lincoln: Pseudohistory, Psychohistory and History* (Urbana, 1988), a publication containing the papers and comments thereon at the 1984 Gettysburg conference; Don E. Fehrenbacher, *Lincoln in Text and Context: Collected Essays* (Stanford, 1987).

8. T. Harry Williams, *Lincoln and His Generals* (New York, 1952); Kenneth P. Williams, *Lincoln Finds a General,* 5 vols. (New York, 1949–59).

9. Carl von Clausewitz, *On War,* translated by Col. James J. Graham, 3 vols. (London, 1911), I, 23; III, 121; Russell F. Weigley, *The American Way of War* (Bloomington, 1973), xvii; Alastair Buchan, *War in Modern Society: An Introduction* (New York, 1968), 81–82.

10. *War of the Rebellion: A Compilation of the Official Records of the Union and Confederate Armies* (Washington, 1880–1901), Series I, Vol. 34, pt. 3, pp. 332–33. Hereinafter cited as *O.R.*

11. T. Harry Williams, *Lincoln and His Generals,* 11.

12. Clausewitz, *On War,* I, xxiii.

13. *Collected Works of Lincoln,* IV, 332.

14. *Ibid.,* IV, 437, 332.

15. *New York Tribune,* May 23, 1862.

16. *Personal Memoirs of U. S. Grant,* 2 vols. (New York, 1885), I, 368.

17. *Collected Works of Lincoln,* V, 426; VI, 257, 281; *Diary of Gideon Welles,* ed. Howard K. Beale, 3 vols. (New York, 1960), I, 370; Dennett, ed., *Lincoln and the Civil War in the Diaries and Letters of John Hay,* 69.

18. *Memoirs of Grant,* I, 368–69; Burke Davis, *Sherman's March* (New York, 1980), 109.

19. *O.R.,* Ser. I, Vol. 17, Pt. 2, p. 150.

20. *Collected Works of Lincoln,* V, 48–49.

21. *Ibid.,* V, 344–46, 350.

22. *Ibid.,* IV, 506.

23. George B. McClellan, *McClellan's Own Story* (New York, 1886), 487–89.

24. Gideon Welles, "The History of Emancipation," *The Galaxy* 14 (Dec. 1872): 842–43.

25. *Ibid.;* David Donald, ed., *Inside Lincoln's Cabinet: The Civil War Diaries of Salmon P. Chase* (New York, 1954), 149–52; *Diary of Gideon Welles,* I, 142–45; John G. Nicolay and John Hay, *Abraham Lincoln: A History,* 10 vols. (New York, 1890), VI, 158–63.

26. The texts of the preliminary and final proclamations are in *Collected Works of Lincoln,* V, 433–36; VI, 28–30.

27. Marcus Spiegel to Caroline Spiegel, Jan. 25, 1863, Jan. 22, 1864, in Frank L. Byrne and Jean Powers Soman, eds., *Your True Marcus: The Civil War Letters of a Jewish Colonel* (Kent, Ohio, 1985), 226, 315–16.

28. *Collected Works of Lincoln,* VI, 408–9. Lincoln was here repeating the words of General Grant (a prewar Democrat) who had written to him on August 23, 1863, in enthusiastic support of emancipation and black troops. (Robert Todd Lincoln Collection of Abraham Lincoln Papers, Library of Congress.)

29. Edward Stanwood, *A History of the Presidency* (Boston, 1903), 301–2; *Collected Works of Lincoln,* VII, 23.

30. Dunbar Rowland, ed., *Jefferson Davis, Constitutionalist: His Letters, Papers, and Speeches,* 10 vols. (Jackson, Miss., 1923), V, 409; *O.R.,* Ser. II, Vol. 5, pp. 797, 940–41.

31. *Collected Works of Lincoln,* VII, 435; Hudson Strode, *Jefferson Davis: Tragic Hero, 1864–1889* (New York, 1964), 77. For the abortive peace negotiations of 1864, see Edward C. Kirkland, *The Peacemakers of 1864* (New York, 1927), chaps. 2–3.

32. *Collected Works of Lincoln,* VIII, 151.

33. *Ibid.,* VII, 499–501, 506–7.

34. *Ibid.,* V, 501, 517; Nicolay and Hay, *Abraham Lincoln,* IX, 221.

35. *Collected Works of Lincoln,* VIII, 151.

36. *Ibid.,* VIII, 279; Strode, *Jefferson Davis,* 140–41.

37. Francis B. Carpenter, *Six Months at the White House with Abraham Lincoln* (New York, 1866), 77.

V. How Lincoln Won the War with Metaphors

1. David M. Potter, "Jefferson Davis and the Political Factors in Confederate Defeat," in David Donald, ed., *Why the North Won the Civil War* (Baton Rouge, 1960), 112, 104.

2. Paul D. Escott, *After Secession: Jefferson Davis and the Failure of Confederate Nationalism* (Baton Rouge, 1978), 269.

3. The metaphor can be found in Roy P. Basler, ed., *The Collected Works of Abraham Lincoln,* 9 vols. (New Brunswick, N.J., 1953–55), IV, 433; the exchange between Lincoln and the government printer was recounted in Francis B. Carpenter, *Six Months at*

the White House with Abraham Lincoln (New York, 1866), 126–27.

4. *Collected Works of Lincoln*, III, 546–47.

5. Carpenter, *Six Months at the White House*, 312–13.

6. *Ibid.*, 235–36; Paul M. Zall, *Abe Lincoln Laughing: Humorous Anecdotes from Original Sources by and about Abraham Lincoln* (Berkeley, 1982), 3.

7. Paraphrased from Carpenter, *Six Months at the White House*, 138–39.

8. Quoted in Herbert Joseph Edwards and John Erskine Hankins, *Lincoln the Writer: The Development of His Literary Style* (Orono, Maine, 1962), 26.

9. Keith Jennison, *The Humorous Mr. Lincoln* (New York, 1965), 26.

10. James M. McPherson, *Ordeal By Fire: The Civil War and Reconstruction* (New York, 1982), 319.

11. *Collected Works of Lincoln*, VI, 249, 273.

12. Zall, *Abe Lincoln Laughing*, 86.

13. Tyler Dennett, ed., *Lincoln and the Civil War in the Diaries and Letters of John Hay* (New York, 1939), 179.

14. Shelby Foote, *The Civil War: A Narrative. Red River to Appomattox* (New York, 1974), 864; *Collected Works of Lincoln*, VII, 499.

15. *Collected Works of Lincoln*, IV, 18.

16. Carpenter, *Six Months at the White House*, 310–11.

17. *Collected Works of Lincoln*, II, 465–66.

18. *Ibid.*, V, 223, 318.

19. Carpenter, *Six Months at the White House*, 20–21.

20. *Collected Works of Lincoln*, V, 350, 343.

21. *Ibid.*, V, 345–46.

22. *Ibid.*, VII, 281; Carpenter, *Six Months at the White House*, 76–77.

23. *Collected Works of Lincoln*, VII, 302.

24. *Ibid.*, VI, 409–10.

25. *Ibid.*, IV, 271.

26. *Ibid.*, V, 537.

27. Edwards and Hankins, *Lincoln the Writer*, p. 89.

28. James Hurt, "All the Living and the Dead: Lincoln's Imagery," *American Literature* 52 (1980–81): 379.

29. Ward Hill Lamon, *Recollections of Abraham Lincoln, 1847–1865* (Chicago, 1895), 171, 175.

30. *Collected Works of Lincoln*, VII, 24–25.

VI. The Hedgehog and the Foxes

1. Isaiah Berlin, *The Hedgehog and the Fox: An Essay on Tolstoy's View of History* (New York, 1966), 1.

2. Harlan Hoyt Horner, *Lincoln and Greeley* (Urbana, 1953), 251–52; Henry Clay Whitney quoted in Waldo W. Braden, *Abraham Lincoln: Public Speaker* (Baton Rouge, 1988), 65.

3. Paul M. Angle, ed., *Herndon's Life of Lincoln* (Cleveland, 1942), 272–73, 270.

4. Roy P. Basler, ed., *The Collected Works of Abraham Lincoln,* 9 vols. (New Brunswick, N.J., 1953–55), VII, 505.

5. Angle, ed., *Herndon's Lincoln,* 238–39.

6. Basler, ed., *Collected Works of Lincoln,* IV, 235–36, 240.

7. *Ibid.,* 236; Tyler Dennett, ed., *Lincoln and the Civil War in the Diaries and Letters of John Hay* (New York, 1939), 19–20.

8. Basler, ed., *Collected Works of Lincoln,* IV, 438–39; V, 537; VII, 23.

9. *New York Tribune,* Nov. 9, 1860.

10. Horner, *Lincoln and Greeley,* 192–93; Greeley to Lincoln, Dec. 22, 1860, Lincoln Papers, Library of Congress. For the debate over what Greeley really meant, see David M. Potter, "Horace Greeley and Peaceable Secession," and "Postscript," in Potter, *The South and the Sectional Conflict* (Baton Rouge, 1968), 219–42; and Thomas N. Bonner, "Horace Greeley and the Secession Movement," *Mississippi Valley Historical Review* 38 (1951): 425–44.

11. Seward to Lincoln, Jan. 27, 1861, Lincoln Papers.

12. Basler, *Collected Works of Lincoln,* IV, 150–51, 154, 183, 155, 172.

13. Glyndon G. Van Deusen, *William Henry Seward* (New York, 1967), 280.

14. Basler, ed., *Collected Works of Lincoln,* IV, 317–18n.

15. *Ibid.,* 316–17.

16. Lincoln Papers.

17. Basler, ed., *Collected Works of Lincoln,* IV, 457–58.

18. *Basler,* V, 292.

19. *New York World,* July 12, 1864; Frank L. Klement, *The Copperheads in the Middle West* (Chicago, 1960), 233.

20. Edward Chase Kirkland, *The Peacemakers of 1864* (New York, 1927), 108.

21. Greeley to Lincoln, July 7, 1864, and Lincoln to Greeley, July 9, 1864, in Basler, ed., *Collected Works of Lincoln,* VII, 435 and n.

22. Greeley to Lincoln, Aug. 8, 1864, Lincoln Papers. For a discussion of this episode, see Horner, *Lincoln and Greeley,* 296–323.

23. Basler, ed., *Collected Works of Lincoln,* VIII, 151.

24. *Ibid.,* VII, 51, 507.

25. *Ibid.,* V, 388.

26. *Ibid.,* III, 92.

27. Braden, *Abraham Lincoln: Public Speaker,* 35–36.

28. Basler, ed., *Collected Works of Lincoln,* IV, 240; II, 274.

29. *Ibid.,* II, 275–76.

30. *Ibid.,* II, 341; IV, 240. When Lincoln made this extemporaneous speech at Independence Hall, he had already been warned of the plot in Baltimore to assassinate him as he passed through; this matter was obviously on his mind.

31. *Ibid.,* IV, 532.

32. *Ibid.,* VII, 281.

33. *Ibid.,* 281–82.

34. *Ibid.,* V, 389. Stephen B. Oates, *Abraham Lincoln: The Man Behind the Myths* (New York, 1984), 112, makes a similar point.

35. Basler, ed., *Collected Works of Lincoln,* VIII, 333.

VII. Liberty and Power in the Second American Revolution

1. *Congressional Globe,* 39 Cong., 2nd Sess. (Jan. 28, 1867), Appendix, p. 78.

2. Madison quoted in Gordon S. Wood, *The Creation of the American Repubic, 1776–1787* (Chapel Hill, 1969), 413; Madison in *Federalist* No. 47 (Modern Library ed., p. 312); Hamilton in *ibid.,* 174. The best analysis of the theme of liberty against power in colonial America is Bernard Bailyn, *The Ideological Origins of the American Revolution* (Cambridge, Mass., 1967).

3. Josiah Quincy, Jr., quoted in John Phillip Reid, *The Concept of Liberty in the Age of the American Revolution* (Chicago, 1988), 36; *The Writings of Thomas Jefferson,* ed. Paul Leicester Ford, 12 vols. (New York, 1892), VII, 289–308; Jackson to John Overton, June 8, 1829, quoted in Robert Remini, *Andrew Jackson and the Bank War* (New York, 1967), 45.

4. James D. Richardson, comp., *Messages and Papers of the Presidents,* 20 vols. (Washington, 1897), VII, 2780–84.

5. John Stuart Mill, *On Liberty* (Harvard Classics ed., New York, 1909), Vol. 25, p. 203; Carlyle quoted in Phillip S. Paludan, *A Covenant with Death: The Constitution, Law, and Equality in the Civil War Era* (Urbana, 1975), 15.

6. Samuel Johnson, "Taxation No Tyranny," in Donald L. Greene, ed., *Samuel Johnson's Political Writings* (New Haven, 1977), 454.

7. Roy P. Basler, ed., *The Collected Works of Abraham Lincoln*, 9 vols. (New Brunswick, N.J., 1953–55), II, 255, 250, 275–76, 461.

8. Alabamians quoted in William L. Barney, *The Secessionist Impulse: Alabama and Mississippi in 1860* (Princeton, 1974), 110; Elijah Petty to his wife, Sept. 11, Nov. 4, 1862, in Norman D. Brown, ed., *Journey to Pleasant Hill: The Civil War Letters of Captain Elijah P. Petty* (San Antonio, 1982), 78, 99.

9. *Collected Works of Lincoln*, IV, 439.

10. *Ibid.*, IV, 268.

11. Quoted in Wood, *Creation of the American Republic*, 23. For a good analysis of the incompatibility of liberty with license, see Reid, *Concept of Liberty*, esp. chap. 4.

12. *Collected Works of Lincoln*, IV, 426.

13. Karl Marx to Friedrich Engels, Oct. 29, Nov. 17, 1862, in Saul K. Padover, ed. and translator, *Karl Marx on America and the Civil War* (New York, 1972), 263, 264.

14. *Collected Works of Lincoln*, II, 250; VII, 302.

15. Isaiah Berlin, "Two Concepts of Liberty," in *Four Essays on Liberty* (New York, 1970), 118–72, esp. 121–31. For a fuller discussion of these concepts of negative and positive liberty, see above, pp. 61–62.

16. Quoted in Norman K. Risjord, *The Old Republicans: Southern Conservatism in the Age of Jefferson* (New York, 1965), 242.

17. *The Works of James Abram Garfield*, ed. Burke A. Hinsdale, 2 vols. (Boston, 1882), I, 249.

18. Quoted in Reid, *Concept of Liberty*, 43.

19. *Proceedings of the National Convention of Colored Men, Held in the City of Syracuse, N.Y., Oct. 4–7, 1864* (New York, 1864), 57–60; *L'Union*, Dec. 30, 1862; *La Tribune de la Nouvelle Orleans*, Jan. 24, 1865.

20. Phillips in *National Anti-Slavery Standard*, May 3, 1865, and *Liberator*, Feb. 10, 1865; Stevens in *Cong. Globe*, 39 Cong., 2nd Sess., pp. 251–53 (Jan. 3, 1867); Dana in *Boston Commonwealth*, June 24, 1865.

21. William M. Wiecek, *The Guarantee Clause of the U.S. Constitution* (Ithaca, 1972), 1–165.

22. Yates in *Cong. Globe*, 41 Cong., 2nd Sess., p. 1327 (Feb. 16, 1870); Davis in *ibid.*, 38 Cong., 1st Sess., Appendix, p. 82 (March 22, 1864); Lawrence in *ibid.*, 41 Cong., 2nd Sess., p. 43 (Jan. 13, 1870).

23. Charles Sumner to Francis Lieber, Oct. 12, 1865, in Edward

L. Pierce, *Memoir and Letters of Charles Sumner*, 4 vols. (Boston, 1877–93), IV, 260; *Cong. Globe*, 39 Cong., 2nd Sess., p. 3976 (July 20, 1866).

24. Robert J. Kaczorowski, *The Politics of Judicial Interpretation: The Federal Courts, Department of Justice and Civil Rights, 1866–1876* (New York, 1985), xiii, 1, 3, and passim. See also Robert J. Kaczorowski, "Revolutionary Constitutionalism in the Era of the Civil War and Reconstruction," *New York University Law Review* 61 (1986): 863–940.

25. *North Carolina Senate Journal, 1866–1867*, quoted in McNeill Smith, "Of the Search for Original Intent: Curtis on the Fourteenth Amendment and the Bill of Rights," *Law and Social Inquiry* 13 (1988): 598–99; *Cong. Globe*, 39th Cong., 1st Sess., p. 2538 and Appendix, p. 134.

26. Richard Yates in *Cong. Globe*, 39th Cong., 1st Sess., Appendix, p. 99 (Feb. 19, 1866); Boston *Commonwealth*, Dec. 25, 1863.

27. *Cong. Globe*, 39th Cong., 1st Sess., p. 570 (Feb. 1, 1866).

28. Representative Jehu Baker of Illinois in *ibid.*, 39th Cong., 1st Sess., Appendix, p. 255 (July 9, 1866); Rep. William Lawrence of Ohio in *ibid.*, 1837 (April 1866); Rep. James A. Garfield of Ohio in *ibid.*, Appendix, p. 67 (Feb. 1, 1866); Sen. Lot Morrill of Maine, *ibid.*, Appendix, p. 155 (March 8, 1866); Sen. Jacob Howard of Michigan, *ibid.*, p. 2766 (May 26, 1866).

29. Swayne in *U.S. v. Rhodes;* Woods in *U.S. v. Hall,* quoted in Kaczorowski, "Revolutionary Constitutionalism," *loc. cit.,* 901, 917.

30. Kaczorowski, *Politics of Judicial Interpretation,* 131.

31. Louis S. Gerteis, *From Contraband to Freedman: Federal Policy Toward Southern Blacks 1861–1865* (Westport, Conn., 1973), 5; John S. Rosenberg, "Toward a New Civil War Revisionism," *American Scholar* 38 (1969): 271, 272, 266. Eric Foner coined the label of "postrevisionist" for this school of historians in "Reconstruction Revisited," *Reviews in American History* 10 (1982): 82–100. For a more detailed discussion and critique of the postrevisionists, see above, pp. 13–22.

32. Eric Foner, *Nothing But Freedom: Emancipation and Its Legacy* (Baton Rouge, 1983); Eric Foner, *Reconstruction: America's Unfinished Revolution 1863–1877* (New York, 1988).

33. *Slaughter-House Cases,* 16 Wallace 36. For an analysis of this case and its ramifications, see Kaczorowski, *Politics of Judicial Interpretation,* 143–66.

34. 16 Wallace 83.

35. Senator George Boutwell of Massachusetts in *Congressional*

Record, 43rd Cong., 1st Sess., p. 4116 (May 21, 1874); Rep. Robert
S. Hale of New York in *ibid.,* 2nd Sess., p. 979 (Feb. 4, 1875).

36. 23 Fed. Cases 710; 92 US. Reports 542.

37. Quoted in Kaczorowski, *Politics of Judicial Interpretation,*
211, 210.

38. Republican leader quoted in William B. Hesseltine, *Ulysses
S. Grant, Politician* (New York, 1935), 358; attorney general quoted
in Richard N. Current, *Those Terrible Carpetbaggers* (New York,
1988), 321.

39. Quoted in Kaczorowski, *Politics of Judicial Interpretation,*
63, 220.

40. Frederic Bancroft, ed., *Speeches, Correspondence and Political Papers of Carl Schurz,* 6 vols. (New York, 1913), I, 487, 502, 488,
489, 490, 495.

41. *Ibid.,* III, 121, 144, 151–52, 141, 130–31, 125.

Index

Davis, Jefferson (cont.)
93–94; literalness of language,
96, 99, 112
DeBow, James B.D., 27
Declaration of Independence, 5,
27, 46, 50, 138; Lincoln on, 24,
51, 54, 115, 126–27
Democratic party, 71; and slavery,
104–5; opposes antislavery war,
31, 42, 82, 85, 88, 124; and civil
liberties issue, 58–59, 63; opposes Fourteenth Amendment
and enforcement, 141–42, 149
Depew, Chauncey, 99
Disraeli, Benjamin, 24
Douglas, Stephen A., 51, 52–53, 54,
104, 126
Douglass, Frederick, 139
Dred Scott case, 48, 59, 105

Early, Jubal, 67–68
Emancipation: Lincoln urges in
border states, 32–34, 83, 86,
105–6; Emancipation Proclamation, 66; Lincoln issues, 34, 43,
83–85, 91, 106–7, 129–30; impact
of, 35, 86–87; Lincoln refuses to
recede from, 88–90, 124. See
also Slavery
Engels, Friedrich, 6
Everett, Edward, 112

Fehrenbacher, Don E., 69
Field, Stephen J., 146
Fifteenth Amendment, 22, 63; and
revolution in constitutionalism,
141, 150
Foner, Eric, 20, 21, 144–45
Fort Donelson, capture of, 77, 78
Fort Henry, capture of, 77, 78
Fort Pickens, 120
Fort Stevens, 67
Fort Sumter: issue of in 1861, 65,
119–20; Confederates attack, 75,
116
Fourteenth Amendment, 22, 63;
passage of, 5; and revolution in
constitutionalism, 141–43; and
Slaughterhouse Cases, 145–47;
and U.S. v. Cruikshank, 147–48
Fox, Gustavus, 119

Franklin, battle of, 90
Frémont, John C., 82, 128, 129

Garfield, James A.: on Civil War as
revolution, 3–5, 19; on reconstruction, 138
Gerteis, Louis, 14
Gettysburg, battle of, 79, 100, 101,
109
Gettysburg Address, Lincoln's, 56,
64, 86, 91, 110–12, 114, 130, 136,
144
Graebner, Norman, 23–24, 41
Grant, Ulysses S., 35, 71, 80; cap-
tures Fort Donelson, 77; battle
of Shiloh, 78; becomes general
in chief, 67–68, 79, 101; Petersburg siege, 87, 102, 122; as president, 150–51
Greeley, Horace, 114; and secession, 117–18; and first battle of
Bull Run, 121; and peace negotiations in 1864, 87–88, 122–24;
and relationship of slavery and
war, 41, 124, 127
Guarantee Clause of the Constitution: and Reconstruction, 140–41

Habeas Corpus, writ of, Lincoln
suspends, 57, 59; and Ku Klux
Klan, 143. See also Civil Liberties
Halleck, Henry W., 35, 66, 70, 80
Hamilton, Alexander, 132
Hammond, James, 50
Hanks, Dennis, 100
Hay, John, 116
Hayes, Rutherford B., 149
Herndon, William, 114, 115
Hinsdale, Burke, 3
Hobbes, Thomas, 135
Holmes, Oliver Wendell, Jr., 67
Hood, John Bell, 90
Hooker, Joseph, 78–79, 100–101
Hunter, David, 82, 129

Jackson, Andrew, 132
Jackson, Thomas J. ("Stonewall"),
66, 78
Jefferson, Thomas, 37, 54; Declaration of Independence, 27, 46, 52,
138; understanding of liberty,

48–49; Kentucky Resolutions, 132; Louisiana Purchase, 133
Johnson, Andrew, 35
Johnson, Reverdy, 149
Johnson, Samuel, 133, 134
Julian, George W., 131, 133, 138

Kaczorowski, Robert J., 141
Kansas-Nebraska Act, 105, 126
Know-Nothings, 53
Ku Klux Klan, 143, 145, 147

Lamon, Ward Hill, 111
Lawrence, William, 141
Lee, Robert E., 68, 78–79, 87, 100–101
Liberal Republican party, 150
Liberty: definitions of, 43–46, 133, 135; American tradition of, 46–47, 131–33, 138; and slavery, 45, 47–54, 56, 61, 107–8, 133–34; Lincoln on, 43–44, 51–54, 63–64, 107–8, 127, 133, 136–37; South secedes in name of, 55, 134–35, 137; Union fights in name of, 55–56; transformation from negative to positive liberty, 61–64, 136–38; and black suffrage, 138–41; and national power in Reconstruction, 131, 133, 140–44; and retreat from positive liberty, 149–52. See also Civil Liberties
Lieber, Francis, 45, 48
Lincoln, Abraham, 144; and black soldiers, 35, 89, 109; and civil liberties, 57–61; urges border states to abolish slavery, 32–34, 83, 86, 105–6; communications skills of, 93–94; and use of parables and metaphors, 95–112; on Declaration of Independence, 24, 115, 126–27; and Emancipation Proclamation, 6, 14, 34, 43, 66, 83–86, 91, 105–7, 124, 129–30; on liberty, 43–45, 51–55, 63–64, 107–8, 136–37; qualities of mind, 114–15; and peace negotiations issue, 88–90, 122–24; on revolution, 24–25, 28, 30, 36–37, 39, 40–42; on slavery, 23, 28, 30–32, 41, 51–52, 81–82, 102–8, 110,

118–19, 124–30, 134–35; and strategy, 65–71, 74–81, 91, 121–22; and unconditional surrender, 87–91; interprets cause of Union, 28–29, 31, 41, 56, 59, 110–11, 113–30, 135–36
Louisiana, Reconstruction in, 150–52

MacArthur, Douglas, 73
McClellan, George B., 67, 100, 101; and Peninsula campaign, 77; Antietam, 78–79; on slavery, 82–83, 85; presidential candidate, 88
Macon, Nathaniel, 137
Madison, James, 131
Manassas (Bull Run), first battle of, 76, 121; second battle of, 78
Marx, Karl, 6, 8, 15, 24
Meade, George G., 79, 101
Mill, John Stuart, 45, 133
Miller, Samuel, 146
Milligan, Lambdin, and *ex parte Milligan*, 58
Moore, Barrington, 9, 11
Morrill, Lot M., 142

Nashville, battle of, 90
Neely, Mark E., Jr., 68
New York Herald, 7
New York Times, 89
New York Tribune, 123, 124; on secession, 27; expects Confederate defeat, 77–78; go-in-peace editorials, 117
New York World, 122
Nicolay, John, 121

Olsen, Otto, 24

Peace negotiations issue, in 1864, 87–89, 122–24; Hampton Roads meeting in 1865, 90
Petersburg, siege of, 68, 87, 102
Phillips, Wendell, 5, 139
Pierce, Franklin, 104, 132
Potter, David M., 93, 112

Randall, James G., 22
Ransom, Roger, 17–18
Raymond, Henry, 89